CHRIS

TA

OFF THE RECORD

CHRIS TARRANT

TARRANT OFF THE RECORD

TALES FROM THE FLIP SIDE

CARTOONS BY
JENNIFER TARRANT

HarperCollins*Publishers*

HarperCollins*Publishers*
77–85 Fulham Palace Road,
Hammersmith, London W6 8JB

A Paperback Original 1997
1 3 5 7 9 8 6 4 2

A catalogue record for this book is
available from the British Library

ISBN 0 00 653023 0

Set in Aldus by
Rowland Phototypesetting Ltd,
Bury St Edmunds, Suffolk

Printed and bound in Great Britain by
Caledonian International Book Manufacturing Ltd, Glasgow

CONTENTS

PREFACE

As we were leaving an extraordinary night on my *This Is Your Life,* one of my kids said to me in all seriousness, 'Dad, why is it that all your friends are absolutely raving mad?'

I have to admit, I've never really thought about it before, but she was absolutely right. Throughout the programme they came on, one after the other, each one ever so slightly more potty than the one before.

My life has been awash with lunatics. My dear old grandad was mad as a march hare. My dad, to this day a very successful businessman, is still a few peas short of a casserole. Even at school it was the weirdest and most deranged children that I always seemed to collect around me.

Alarmingly, many of them grew up to be captains of British industry – one's a Harley Street surgeon; another now works in New York as a psychiatrist; and one's in jail. In my TV reporting days, I was positively encouraged to go out and find seriously daft people to interview night after night. On *Tiswas* and *OTT*, we deliberately cultivated them. Week after week, people would come in as our guests who had just arrived from the planet Zarg.

Since I came to work at Capital Radio in London in 1984, they've followed me in droves: wall to wall nutters

who have at last found their own little radio home. My kids are right: I'm surrounded by mad men and even madder women. But without them, my life would not have been as rich and varied. I wouldn't have had anything like as much fun and I'd probably still be driving lorries or teaching in London's East End.

I once spent eight hours interviewing a man walking from Worcester to Eversham who had four ferrets down the front of his trousers. I spent another whole day soothing a man who had a live pigeon on his head. He even went to bed with it still there. I filmed a guy called Jake, who preached to the local sheep from a specially contructed pulpit on his roof. And it's people like him that litter the pages of this book.

The woman who wanted to have babies with a gorilla; the pike that ate a horse and cart; the waiter who didn't realize that lager has an alcoholic content; a guy who danced to the flute with live rats down his see-through tights; the world champion egg, nose and water jumper; the man who jumped out of a window live on the radio! You'll meet them all here, and I hope you enjoy them as much as I have. My life and the company I've kept has teetered on the brink of sheer insanity for years . . . and I've loved every minute of it.

Chris Tarrant

CHRIS TARRANT

TARRANT OFF THE RECORD

Finger Flickin' Good

As a kid, you have little or no chance of comparing your experiences with those of other kids outside your immediate circle of playmates. So you tend to assume that everybody else's lives and habits are identical to your own. If there are a dozen kids out of twenty in your class who all breed rattlesnakes for pets and come to school on white rhinos, you just naturally assume that that's about the national average. Nobody ever tells you you're in a nut house.

My dad's called Basil and I grew up assuming there were thousand of kids out there with dads called Basil. Only, of course, there weren't. No one in their right mind is called Basil. I've only ever heard of two other Basils in my entire life: one is Basil Fawlty and one is Basil Brush. And you wouldn't want either of them as your dad, would you? Basil Tarrant is a strange cross between the two.

His best friend was called Pomeroy. Uncle Pom to us kids. I've certainly never heard of another Pomeroy anywhere in the whole wide world. But as a little kid, I just thought there were Basils and Pomeroys everywhere.

It was the same for me with Finger Flicking. I just assumed that that was what everybody else was doing all over the world, or certainly all over the British Isles.

It was all Mr Wormwell's fault – or Major Wormwell

as he insisted on being called at least twenty years after the cessation of all Second World War hostilities. I've since had a lot of doubts about whether he actually ever went anywhere more dangerous than Basingstoke. Anyway, the Major was the headmaster of this very twee little school that my mum and dad decided to pack me off to as soon as I was big enough to see over a desk and sit on a lavatory without a serious risk of drowning. On that first day at school, the Major initiated me into Finger Flicking.

He announced something like, 'As this is the first day of term, you can all have the afternoon off,' and all the six and seven-year-olds around me started waving their arms in the air like helicopters. Even the Major joined in. I quickly learned that this was what you did at school when you were pleased about something.

To define the flicking action more precisely, you press together the thumb and middle finger of each hand and then, with the rest of your fingers splayed open and your elbows bent so that your hands are about level with your shoulders, you wave your hands back and forth from the wrist as fast as possible. (Note: At this point of the book you will get odd looks from the people around you and will probably be asked to go somewhere else!)

When done by a whole school of children at morning assembly the noise can be deafening. But at my nice little school it happened a lot. Sometimes, if the news just brought delight to one individual, he would stand there happily flicking away all on his own. No embarrassment whatsoever, it was just what you did.

'Well done, Tarrant. You've only just turned nine and you've got all three letters right in "cat".'

'Thank you, Sir.'

Flick, flick, flick!

We all did it at the slightest hint of happiness. Indeed, until I was twelve I regularly flicked two or three times a week: sometimes on my own, sometimes with just a couple of close friends, sometimes with the whole school and the headmaster. Naturally I assumed that this was going on all over British classrooms. I didn't know Major Wormwell was completely out of his mind, did I?

At the age of twelve, when I moved on to big school, I was in for a series of shocks. The first was that I was no longer the most important boy in the whole wide

world, head and captain of absolutely everything. I was an insignificant little worm, and if I ever forgot it regular reminders were handed out by much, much bigger boys in the form of fairly savage beatings.

The other shocking lesson I quite vividly remember learning on the first Monday morning assembly I attended. Term had been in progress for less than a week, but over the weekend our First XV rugby team had stuffed it up some other little bunch of Hooray Henries by something like sixty points to nil and the headmaster was absolutely delighted.

'A marvellous start,' he told the whole school. 'A result we can all be justly proud of.'

(The fact that the First XV wouldn't get a single A-level between them and only one of them could do joined up writing was not thought to be important.)

It was a great moment for all the boys to share in and, of course, absolutely delighted for my new friends, I started waving my little arms and flicking my fingers like there was no tomorrow.

Whirr . . . whirr . . . whirr. Flick, flick, flick I went, along with the other 800 happy boys at my new school. Only, after about thirty seconds, I realized that the others weren't all joining in. In fact, none of them were doing it at all. Including masters, there were 1,638 eyes all trained on this odd little fair-haired kid in the first form who had something seriously wrong with the ends of his fingers.

It was only as I was being dragged out of my place by my ears and dumped outside the headmaster's study to

await his displeasure (which turned out to be six very crisp ones across the backside for being a disruptive influence) that I understood how unique had been Major Wormwell's way of expressing true happiness.

The Nice Little Old Ladies

I was once asked to give away the annual prizes at an Over Fifties Ladies' Club down in Sussex. It seemed an unlikely booking but, basically, because there was a few quid in it, I happily agreed to go along.

They were very nice; all blue rinses and dresses like tablecloths. I was made very welcome and sat contentedly sipping wine until it was my turn to do my bit. I managed a fairly gentle speech, gave away prize fruit bowls and hair-do tokens to nice little old ladies who'd done the most knitting or made the best pickle or scored the most goals, and sat down to enjoy the rest of the evening.

The chairwoman thanked all the ladies for their hard work during the past year, thanked me and then, just before the buffet got under way, asked us to welcome the folk group.

Now I don't know who these three lads were but what followed was one of the funniest things I ever saw. They did a couple of Spinners' numbers, and then got us all ready to join in the chorus of the next one.

'This is marvellous fun,' all the nice little old ladies agreed, eager for a singalong.

The next number was called 'A Gentle Tribute to the Great Network of Waterways That Criss-Cross Our Beautiful Land' and, after the first quiet verse, a whole church hall full of totally innocent little old ladies went eagerly straight into the chorus:

'Far canal, far canal
Take out your dinghy
Do your own thingy
And sail up that far canal.
Oh far canal,
Oh far canal,
Sail up that far canal . . .'

And to cries of 'everybody' and 'one more time', with me sitting there not daring to look anyone in the eye, one hundred dear little old ladies all sang chorus after chorus after chorus at the tops of their voices:

'Far canal, oh far canal . . .'

Alternative Accommodation

For four very happy months of my life I lived in a mini van. I'm not quite sure how it actually happened. I remember having a fairly spectacular bust-up with my then girlfriend and roaring off into the night, only to find after about forty miles of furious driving that I hadn't got anywhere to go.

ALTERNATIVE ACCOMMODATION

It was winter in south-east London. I was teaching English to a motley collection of very large West Indians, East Indians, Cypriots, Turks, Greeks, Italians, Irish and traditional English skinheads. English lessons were spent wrestling with the intellectual dilemmas posed by the full stop, and the more human dilemmas of who'd set light to Thompson's hair, and when were they going to put him out?

As you can imagine, the domestic backgrounds of the students were varied to say the least, so the fact that 'Sir' lived in a mini van outside the school didn't bother them much. After an initial confrontation when two of them jacked me up on bricks while I lay happily dozing inside, it all worked out very well. I was awakened one night by one of my little lads clanking about under the bonnet.

'Just borrowing your battery, Sir, to start my mate's Cooper 'S' – promise it'll be back before assembly.'

And sure enough it was.

It was a bit cramped doing my marking in the evenings so I usually did that in the pub instead, but generally it was very cosy. I had a mattress, pillow, blankets and my own little alarm clock called Johnston, who used to knock on the windscreen at 7.30 every morning. I would then dive into the school for a nice shower and, when all the other already stressed-out staff crawled in from all over the south of England, grumbling about traffic jams and British Rail, I'd be fresh as a daisy.

The ultimate achievement was getting the Post Office to deliver my mail to me. After several weeks of

hassle with the GPO head office, the first delivery was magic. There was a scratching on the thick ice on the windscreen and a voice enquiring 'Mr Tarrant?' As I slid open the little window there was the proof on the envelope:

C. J. Tarrant, Esq.
161 GLO
Sprules Road
London SE4

In the end I had to give the van up because my love life had more or less come to a standstill. Conversations like, 'Shall we go back to your place?', 'Well, actually, we're in it', I could handle, and most of the ladies in question came to terms with the idea that 'popping upstairs' meant climbing over the seat into the back. I

suspect several of them had been through that routine before.

What really seemed to put them off was having to sit with the kettle and the lighted blow-lamp on their knees when they wanted a cup of coffee.

The Opening Ceremony

For no reason that I, as a mere hireling, ever really understood, my bosses at Capital Radio – having made millions and trillions, year after year, originally out of running one radio station, then two radio stations, then half the radio stations in Britain, Europe and, of all places, India – decided to go into the restaurant trade.

We moved from our dilapidated old premises round the corner from Euston Station to a glittering new multi-storey, hi-tech studio complex right in the middle of Leicester Square. A new merchandising shop was built at the front so that bewildered Japanese tourists could take home pictures of me to impress their bemused children with. They also decided that a really wacko money-making wheeze would be to set up a themed radio cafe right across the bottom half of the building, underneath the studios, and enter into head-to-head competition with such culinary legends as Planet Hollywood, the Hard Rock Cafe and Spud-U-Like. It was all very exciting. In fact the bosses became so excited that they then spent a further huge sum of money buying a whole chain of restaurants all around the world.

This was of course great news for all us simple souls who put the records on. None of us really understood it but we did suddenly feel part of a great international brotherhood and it does mean, for example, that I can get discount whenever I'm in the bar that we now apparently own in the Lebanon. Whether or not the eight-foot bearded Hesbollah waiter will accept my Capital discount voucher remains to be seen!

Anyway, the first job was officially to open the initial venture – the Capital Radio Cafe in Leicester Square. A glittering bash was publicized. Every stretch limousine in London was booked for a bit of shameless showing off, all the DJs were squeezed into their ill-fitting shiny suits. All sorts of celebrities and pop stars turned up, along with a lot of journalists anxious for any wicked little story that they could get their hands on. I was having a few beers at the bar and was blissfully unaware that the wickedest story of them all was unfolding behind the scenes – namely that George Michael, with whom Capital have always had a great relationship, had at the very last minute, for whatever reason, pulled out of being the Cafe's official opener and ribbon cutter.

It was such a closely guarded secret that most of us didn't even know that he was scheduled to do it in the first place. But of course all the tabloid journalists knew, and they were loving the drama of his non-arrival.

I got a message to pop round and see my bosses so,

beer in hand, I wandered round behind the scenes to find them all looking distinctly ill at ease.

The Managing Director said to me, 'Chris – I wonder if you could do me a favour? Somebody's let us down so could you please do a quick official opening for us?'

So I said, 'Okay', and walked back to the reception – like a lamb to the slaughter.

All the other pop stars and their managers had understandably hidden behind the pillars for fear of being asked to do the honours, so there was just me and Tamara Beckwith (not like her to be available for a photographic opportunity!) left to do the official business and cut through the ribbon. I should have realized that I'd been set up as I walked down through the floodlights to the microphone and saw a piano waiting by the ribbon. Only as I was making the speech did Mick Brown, one of my DJ mates, whisper in my ear to reveal to me the full

enormity of whose shoes I was filling. I got through the speech as quickly as I could and declared the place officially open to polite applause.

It was only as I was turning away and there was a brief, rather embarrassed silence that one of the gentlemen of Her Majesty's press shouted out, 'So you're not going to do *Careless Whisper* then?'

Don't Touch the Nose

I used to work at Central TV back in the seventies and was filming for them one week down in Herefordshire. It was diabolical weather, bitter cold and pouring with rain most of the day, which made life pretty miserable and filming downright impossible. After about four days of hanging about our hotel, getting smashed out of our brains every night and soldiering through the same menu every lunch and dinnertime, I was invited by a very nice lady I had interviewed one morning to have dinner with her and her husband, just to break the monotony. I accepted very gratefully.

I spruced myself up and knocked on their very large front door at 7.30 on the dot. A smiling Patricia came out to meet me, produced a large scotch from their antique drinks' cabinet and motioned me into the lounge.

'Charles is by the fire,' she said. 'Go in and say hello while I serve up, but whatever you do, don't touch his nose.'

I stared incredulously after her departing back, my mouth opening and closing. What? Don't touch his nose? It had never crossed my mind. Why on earth would I go up to a complete stranger and touch his nose?

I went into the lounge and there, beaming amiably in front of the fire, was Charles. He was a great big bear of a man, about six foot five, used to play rugby for London Welsh, terribly well spoken and kindness itself.

'Nice to meet you, Chris,' he said. 'Got a drink, have you? Good. Come and sit down.'

Now, all this polite chatting and handshaking was all very well and I made suitably innocuous replies, but really and truly all I wanted to ask him about was his nose. What was wrong with it? Why couldn't I touch it? I kept staring at it. It looked all right to me. A little large perhaps but not broken or anything, no sign of a bandage.

Then the food arrived, which was excellent, particularly after the meagre fare I'd been getting at the hotel. The wine flowed freely and we all got on like rabbits in a field of wet turnips. Charles had a really silly sense of humour and his wife was lovely. But all the time, in the back of my mind, I kept hearing Patricia's words of warning, ringing in my brain over and again:

'Whatever you do, don't touch the nose.'

The whole thing was absurd. Perhaps I'd misheard her. Perhaps she'd said 'rose' or 'hose', but that was even sillier. 'Don't touch his rose', 'Don't touch his hose'. No – I definitely hadn't misheard, and although nothing had been further from my mind when I walked into their house that evening, by the end of dinner I wanted to touch

Charles's nose more than anything else in the world.

The brandy came round, the cigars came out, Charles and I sat closely together, roaring with laughter and slapping each other on the back until, eventually, about two o'clock in the morning, I could restrain myself no longer. As Charles sat rocking with laughter in his chair, I reached across the table, gently grabbed both nostrils between thumb and forefinger, and gave it a damn good tweaking.

There was a scream from Patricia and a crash of broken glass. Charles let out the roar of a wounded elephant, there was a flash in front of my face and I vaguely made out the shape of a huge hairy fist coming towards me.

The next thing I remember is lying on the floor under the dining table, with the taste of blood in my mouth and a terribly apologetic Charles looming over me, saying, 'I'm really terribly sorry, old boy, but surely Patricia warned you . . . ?'

Breakfast in America

A couple of years ago I did a week of 'Breakfasts in America'. To be more specific, I did a very frenetic, mind numbing but absolutely fascinating week of being the morning guest of the day on breakfast radio shows across the States. I was introduced in various ways, including 'The hottest thing to come out of London, England (pronounced 'Ing-land') since the Duchess of York'! I didn't know whether to be flattered or insulted! But compared

to radio in the UK it was like visiting another planet. I was exhausted just watching them.

3.55 on a bitter, cold, snowy morning at WPLJ in New York and Scott Shannon is already in the studio with the rest of his breakfast show team going through the morning papers, dreaming up ideas for a phone-in, even writing and recording sketches for God's sake! At 3.55 a.m.? They're not even on air until 6 a.m. yet the scene is typical of literally thousands of radio stations all over the USA. I'm not sure if the end product is necessarily any better than ours, but they certainly work harder. But then, being Americans, they just would, wouldn't they?

At many stations even the men in suits are there at that ungodly hour, having pre-breakfast show meetings. And after they all sign off air wearily at ten o'clock, there's none of this 'Have a great Tuesday, see you tomorrow morning' and diving off into the Mercedes business. Oh no. They all get dragged off for yet another meeting and maybe, on a really good day, yet another meeting after that.

So fierce is the competition for ratings that many of their disc jockeys seem to get home when it's just about time to get up again

I have done the Capital FM breakfast show in London for over ten years now and I have to admit shamefacedly that I do not get into the studio at four o'clock in the morning. Mind you, nor do any of the grey men in suits. When they do stroll in from their country seats, it's usually just nicely in time for pre-lunch drinky-poos. Of course I'm only repeating what I've heard from

some of the other DJs. Personally, I've long gone by then.

If I'm parking my car as I hear the opening jingle start playing at 6.29 and a half, that's always seemed about right to me. I'm pretty sure I speak for almost all the rest of the fine body of breakfast DJs in Britain, too. I remember once listening to Kenny Everett do a very funny first twenty minutes of his show on the car phone as he was still driving in. If he'd done that in New York, he'd probably have been hung from the Empire State Building for the crows to pick his eyes out . . . just as a warning to others.

The only US DJ I came across who doesn't linger around for yet another meeting after his show is over is Tom Joyner, the morning man at KKDA in Dallas. It's not that he's lazy – far from it – it's just that after fronting the breakfast show in Dallas he has to fly straight off to do the afternoon show in Chicago. That's like me signing off in London at ten o'clock, saying, 'I'll see you tomorrow morning at 6.30 – I'm just off to Leningrad.'

Of course the rewards for the top DJs are very high. Probably fifty or so of America's main morning DJs earn over five million dollars a year. But there are hundreds of other very good ones who work equally hard on surprisingly meagre contracts. It's all down to advertisers and sponsors and of course those wretched ratings. It's the same in the UK, but not on quite the same savage scale. With commercial radio opening up more and more in Britain there are now nearly forty stations in London alone – in Los Angeles there are ninety-four and in New

York there are twelve! New ones are opening all the time. Old ones are going bust all the time.

Stations will try anything and everything to get advertising. One fifteen-minute segment I heard in Washington was sponsored by a local cats' home. The news on another station was 'brought to you by the best funeral parlour in town'. The best known DJ in Los Angeles, Mr Rick Dees at Kiss FM, has a huge billboard of himself at the top of a skyscraper, dominating almost as much of the LA skyline as the famous Hollywood sign on the hills.

It carries the simple message, 'Did you hear what Rick said today?'

Another station erected a huge video screen over a main road junction so that you could actually watch the DJs in their studio while listening to them on your car radio. This experiment was brought to an abrupt end by the traffic police after a string of cars bumped into each other as their drivers were staring up at the video screens . . . At the cheaper end of the market, Washington WRXQ – a company with rather less to spend – had their traffic guy out on the streets with a sandwich board round his neck plugging the name of the station, recruiting new listeners and getting them to talk to the studio live on his little portable phone.

The promotions to get more listeners are endless. One FM station in Los Angeles gave a lady a million dollars for knowing her birthday. Another elderly lady, who couldn't even drive, won a brand new $90,000 Porsche. A man in Tennessee won a free car-wash for life, and a lady in Atlanta won a golden retriever. Many FM stations over

the last twelve months have been regularly giving away tummy tucks and breast implants! Apparently, one lady only got half of a two-part question right – so, presumably, she now proudly sports just the one huge silicone breast and the other is still as nature intended.

At WGCI Chicago, Doug Banks – a huge amiable black guy who ate more during the breakfast show that I sat in on than most people eat in a year – was getting listeners to guess what flavour soup he was eating. If they got it right they won cash. If they got it wrong presumably Doug was able to spend more money on even more food!

There was a particularly fine moment during Doug's show when he announced the number of the 'car of the day' for that morning – 'Dial WGCI inside thirty minutes and you win fifty dollars' – only to have a worried policewoman on the line saying she'd been listening to the show, had checked her computer, and discovered that the 'car of the day' was in fact stolen.

There are a lot more women disc jockeys in the States, although only four or five of them are actually the main presenter of their own breakfast show. Mary Glen Lassiter at WGFX Nashville is one of them, and somehow combines being a full-time mum with the gruelling schedule they all have to keep. When I arrived, she'd been up half the night with one of her kids being sick and yet was still back in the studio at 4 a.m., deftly battling off some very strange sounding hillbillies, all hoping to be chosen for telling 'the best joke of the week', contributions to which competition mainly seemed to be jokes about condoms and vibrators. Mary thanked them all for calling and just

kept smiling through until she could race back home and nurse her kid.

Just a few miles down the road from where Mary was fending off the relentless stream of heavy breathers, another station was playing 'a non-stop, back to back hour of your favourite Christian tunes'!

The pace is hysterical. One guy in Georgia had signs propped up in front of him, presumably written by someone in management, saying, 'energy, enthusiasm, excitement – keep it up, non-stop!'

Stations have their own refined slogans like: 'We are the fine dining station – for those who eat their young', 'We are the frequency of delinquency' and 'If you're in the car with someone who doesn't want to listen to KR&R – make the mothers get out and walk'.

To keep up the terrifying pace I couldn't help but notice that some of the DJs took strange potions before they went on air. At 3.55 a.m. one guy was busy shovelling something that clearly was not talcum powder up his nostril. At 4 a.m. he sounded terrific but he looked like death and it all seemed a far cry from David Jacobs and Terry Wogan.

The great thing about American music radio is that there's something for everybody in every town – top forty stations, country stations, 'dusties' (this apparently means very old records with dust on), easy listening, gospel, reggae, non-stop rap, hard rock, soft rock, 'Hispanic middle of the road' – there's always something else just along the FM band. One station only does non-stop twenty-four-hour traffic reports – at 2 a.m. on a Bank

Holiday morning it must make absolutely riveting listening!

For years American stations led the world in the way they presented music radio but the trend in many cities is now moving back to non-stop talk radio. Some of the most successful shows in the States now don't play any music at all – the hosts just talk and talk and talk. Some don't even punctuate it with news or weather, they just keep talking and talking – either to the people on the phones, or often it seems to just anybody who's out there and cares to listen. Particularly at breakfast, when most people don't have time to listen, this seems a very strange concept and one that has never yet really worked in the UK, but on several US stations it's a hugely successful format.

The strangest phenomenon of all on American breakfast radio at present is Howard Stern at XRL New York. He talks non-stop every morning for four hours and manages to be solidly offensive to just about everybody for the whole period. He slags just about everyone: all the other stations, all the other disc jockeys, everyone on television. The whole show is laced with four-letter words, he insults all his guests and talks relentlessly about the size of his willy. He also seems obsessed with oral sex. His other party piece seems to be bad mouthing people with serious illness or physical defects. Funny, I don't find him, but the latest audience figures confirm Howard Stern again as the number one DJ out of the 120 stations in New York.

Not many of the talk radio show hosts seem to worry

too much about who they offend. Politicians, religious orders, racial and sexual minorities are all fair targets to some of these guys. They just can't wait for another day to dawn so that they can get back to ranting away over their live microphones. Subjects are openly explored and people attacked in a way that would have any station taken off the air over here in the UK.

Yet America being America, it operates its own unofficial but very effective form of censorship – at least with some of the more extreme talk show hosts. In recent years, several have been shot dead.

The Bucket of Water Song

At the height of *Tiswas*'s fame in the late seventies, Barry Manilow look-alike and former *Scaffold* group member John Gorman came trotting into the office one day with a song that he'd just penned. It was a pleasant little marching ditty called 'The Bucket of Water Song' and for the next couple of years the thing was to take over our lives. The song worked on the simple premise that when you came to certain key words, like 'bucket of water', for example, you and everyone else around you poured buckets of water all over each other's heads.

We tried it tentatively the next Saturday on *Tiswas* and it was an immediate sensation. After the show the switchboard was jammed with people asking where they could buy the record, although at that stage no such thing existed. By Monday lunchtime we'd heard from people all over the country who had been drenching each other in pubs, clubs and even the washroom at Euston Station, in time to whatever they could remember of the words. Not that the lyrics mattered much: what really mattered was that the song provided yet another excuse for normally perfectly sane, boring grown-ups to behave like great big over-grown children. By the time we repeated the song the next weekend, a whole new social phenomenon had been born . . . bucketing.

From all over the country we heard reports of hundreds of premises flooded out by the occupants as they poured plastic buckets, tin buckets, fire buckets and even sick buckets all over each other in the time to the music. And, of course, because it was all our fault we got it worst of all. For the whole of that lunatic summer everywhere we went people came trotting up either with sploshing receptacles of their own, intended for use on us, or else would ask very politely, 'I know it's a bit of a cheek and I know it's your evening off, but would you mind pouring the contents of the fish tank all over my head, please?'

In a nice quiet restaurant in Brighton, a very refined looking lady poured the contents of an ice bucket all over Sally James's head – just for the sheer fun of it. How we laughed.

The social implications of what we'd stumbled upon were mind blowing. The record release was the next logical step, and although a lot of discos banned it because of the trouble it caused in elegant nightclubs and the damage it did to elegant carpets, it sold in large quantities.

THE BUCKET OF WATER SONG

We were booked for a tour of British theatres and colleges that summer with a rather hurriedly chucked together a show of sorts called '*Tiswas* the Road Show', so the song couldn't have arrived at a better time. The management at Central TV became particularly difficult and miserly about the huge percentage of the gate they would want from each show for the use of the word 'Tiswas', so we changed our name to 'The Four Bucketeers'. This was a bit of a puzzle in itself, because there were actually five of us.

The song became a huge hit and was our anthem up and down the country, and Central never got a quid.

Every night the end of the show was the same. We always had a huge tank, a hose pipe and a large range of buckets organized at the side of the stage. As the music started up we would frantically get rid of everything plugged into the mains and march back out onto the stage, as if for an encore. On this cue, the entire frenzied audience would race out of their seats and wedge themselves against the front of the stage, screaming for a soaking. The scenes were truly fantastic, and yet they became so commonplace to us night after night that we just took them for granted. As we literally threw bucket after bucket of water over the roaring audience, their screams were invariably the same.

'Me, me, oh please, please, me, me, me!'

And the standard plea that we heard at least once every night: 'Oh, please, please, I've paid five pounds for my ticket and I'm still dry.'

Bull in a Nudist Camp

One of my more bizarre filming projects at Central was three days in a nudist camp somewhere in deepest Sussex. God knows what the pretext was. I think it was just an excuse for the producer to spend seventy-two pervy hours ogling all shapes and sizes of women scampering about starkers.

Whatever my expectations of a nudist camp were, there is nothing on earth that could have prepared me for it. When the seven men and one woman of my crew all arrived to check in, the sight of a quite hideous, grossly overweight old battle-axe waiting to greet us at reception with not a stitch on nearly made us all jump back into our cars and drive home in a panic. But there was no turning back.

For the first evening we tried to pretend that it was the most natural thing in the world to be surrounded by naked breasts, buttocks and pubic hair. We tried desperately hard not automatically to stare down at everybody we were introduced to. It's very hard, in fact it's almost impossible to maintain eyeball to eyeball contact. Sooner or later, and usually sooner, your eyes are forced down to the private parts, followed immediately by a guilty jerking of the head back up to meet their gaze, accompanied by a bright reddening of the cheeks.

Of course, the regular nudists have seen it all before and so it got to the point, after only three or four hours,

when we became the ones feeling terribly conspicuous in our clothes. None of the nudists were at all fazed by our being fully dressed, but we began to feel thoroughly uncomfortable and downright silly. And of course it was the girl among us who just had to be the first to get her kit off. We'd all worked with Jane – our PA – for several years and, frankly, had often daydreamed, and on occasion night-dreamed, about seeing her naked. But when she came wandering in dressed only in a clipboard and a stop-watch, all the blokes went terribly red and started staring stupidly at the ceiling.

Although Jane had always been very attractive to all of us, and was magnificent with nothing on, the mystery was gone. In fact the one thing you quickly realized is that a hint of stocking top or a sneaky glimpse down a peeping cleavage is one thing. Total nakedness is something altogether else . . . and sexy it certainly ain't!

Nevertheless, shamed by Jane, we all slowly began to get our kit off. It was a very odd moment. I'd worked with the same crew for several years, but of course I'd never seen their willies, and I sincerely hoped they'd never seen mine. We all tried to carry on as if it was the most natural thing in the world but, frankly, we felt bloody ridiculous. You find yourself doing silly things, like looking for your car keys that are normally in your trouser pocket and suddenly realizing that you haven't even got any trousers, let alone pockets. So you're left doing a rather strange slapping and stroking motion on the top of your thighs, which looks obscene but is better than

the shame of admitting that you are hunting for keys in trousers that are no longer there!

It was a very strange three days, but the filming went well. We had the added amusement of the director who kept sitting on a huge cane chair which left unmistakable marks on his bare buttocks. Whenever he stood up we all giggled uncontrollably behind his back.

Some of the statistics that we discovered were extraordinary. For example, nakedness is, if you'll pardon the expression, on the up and up in this country. Over 30,000 people from every walk of life scamper about in the altogether at the weekends, in spite of the British climate and in spite of a real lack of decent places to go. Our nudist resort was magnificent: an old country house with spectacular walled gardens and an ornamental lake.

Mainly, though, nudists have to meet in places like church halls and leisure centres. Apparently it's the sheer pleasure of 'letting God's good air get to your naked body' that is the attraction.

It's very healthy and all the nudists had all-over tans, while we remained pathetically white throughout our brief visit. There was a lot of sporting good fun, although you had to be a bit discriminating – tennis, football and volleyball were all extra invigorating with your bits and pieces swinging free, but all of us said a firm 'No thank you' to archery and darts!

One of the regular nudists told me the most extraordinary fact of all as we wandered through the open farmland around us. God knows how the researchers found this out

– it must have taken a particular kind of courage to perform this very brave but distinctly foolish experiment. Apparently they discovered that a naked man can safely walk across a bull's field, but when a fully-clothed one tries to set foot on his territory the bull goes raving mad and tries very hard to stick his sharp horns into your soft, squidgy bits.

I desperately wanted to find out why, but I wasn't brave enough to experiment myself. I really do feel that it's up to those who study the animal world to come up with an answer. Of course I'm not suggesting that we should send a shivering and starkers Sir David Attenborough out into the field with a two-ton snorting Aberdeen Angus behind him, but there must be a good reason why the bull doesn't charge.

Having only too clearly seen the average bull's superb mating tackle, perhaps when confronted by the average,

or even bigger than average, naked man he just feels sorry for him! Or, even worse, Mr Bull is incapable of chasing the naked man – because he's helpless with laughter!

Guess Who I've Had in the Back of My Cab?

I suppose that if you're six foot two with silly flaxen hair and you do what I do for a living, for as long as I've done it for a living, you have to get used to being recognized. It's not a problem, it comes with the territory and, in the main, people are very nice, if occasionally confused.

You get used to people saying things like, 'You look just like you do . . .', 'You look nothing like you do . . .', 'You're much taller than you are . . .', 'You're much better looking on the radio . . .'

My absolute favourite encounter was when a complete stranger, a very nice polite woman, came up to me and said, 'You're one of my biggest fans.'

As I say, being approached isn't a problem, but people do sometimes get it terribly wrong. There was a man in the fish market in Birmingham who was convinced that I was Duncan Norvelle. There was a sweet little girl in Southampton who thought I was Geoffrey from *Rainbow* and a clearly dotty woman at Heathrow who was convinced I was Eamonn Andrews: this, despite the fact that dear old Eamonn had been dead for years.

I once walked into a paper shop in Manchester, and as

I came up to the counter the owner, an Indian gentleman, squealed with delight and said, 'It's you, it's you, Sir, off the TV, isn't it?', shook me excitedly by the hand and ran off to get the rest of his family. His wife and several kids appeared and took it in turns to shake me again and again by the hand, while grinning at me and shouting happily at each other in what I think was probably Urdu. It was all very well, but all I really wanted to do was get my paper and beat a polite but hasty retreat.

What happened next, however, was bewildering. The father and mother left the kids still happily jabbering away at me in a language that I had no comprehension of whatsoever, and then returned proudly with a whole collection of antiques – a beautiful bone china tea set, an engraved snuff box, a gold watch on a chain and a magnificent oil painting – all of which they wanted me to value.

I somehow bluffed my way through the whole thing, putting prices on goods that were a complete guess and probably inaccurate by hundreds of pounds, but it was the least I could do and the only way I could get out alive.

I never did get my paper and, to this day, I've absolutely no idea who they thought I was.

Taxi drivers are the worst of all. We've all had the ones who do the 'Guess who I've had in the back of my cab' routine, and they reel off a list of everybody remotely famous who's ever travelled in their taxi, from Barbra Streisand to a bloke who once appeared in the background on *Brookside*. But there's also a particular look that taxi

drivers give you in their mirror if they recognize you. It's a sort of 'I know who you are but I'm not going to disturb you' look, which consists of a strange manic winking every time you stop at traffic lights. They also do an even more peculiar head jerking motion over their shoulder when they my pass other cab drivers as if to communicate, 'Look who I've got in the back of *my* cab.' It's a very odd ritual and can be dangerous at high speed.

Anyway, a bloke was doing this to me all the way across the city a few months ago, as I was on my way over to London Weekend Television for a meeting. I kept my eyes firmly down on my bits of paper, while via the mirror the driver in the front kept winking and twitching his eyes towards me. When I got out I handed him five quid, which he promptly gave back to me and shook me warmly by the hand.

'No, no, no,' he said. 'I wouldn't dream of it. Please have this ride for free, on behalf of myself, my wife and my kids. It's just a way of saying thank you for all the entertainment you've provided over the years on TV, in the newspapers and magazines, on the radio . . . and, above everything, thanks for all the marvellous work you've done at Stoke Mandeville.'

I didn't have the heart to disillusion him and walked into the studios with a big cigar in my mouth, while he shouted out of the window, 'Be lucky, Jim!'

We're Mad As Hell and We Just Won't Take It Any More

In my duties as a news reporter for ATV, I once covered a story about an angry farmer who was in court after taking the law into his own hands and spraying council offices with four tons of cow dung because planners had refused to let him build a bungalow.

He had arrived at his local planning office in Northumberland with his muck spreader and told the housing office exactly what he thought of them. The walls and windows were absolutely covered and he even managed to give a coating to the chairs, computers and carpets inside. Furious officials tried to stop him but were trapped by a ten-inch deep moat of manure.

Grandfather Dave said, 'I must say I felt a lot better afterwards.'

The sixty-three-year-old was convicted of criminal damage, but walked free from court with only an order to pay costs and compensation.

Obviously I can't really condone people taking the law into their own hands. It would undermine the very fabric of our society – but I have to say that sometimes there's nothing like it for sheer satisfaction. There are times when, like Peter Finch in *Network*, 'We're mad as hell and we're just not going to take it anymore.' There are times when the tiny minded, the bullying bureaucrats or

the good old fashioned jobsworths just have to be put in their place.

On a minor scale, I've done it in a supermarket where, having queued for half an hour with two huge baskets of shopping, some idiot at the checkout wouldn't let me have the one beer in amongst it all, and told me very forcefully to put it back on the shelf as they weren't licensed to sell alcohol until six o'clock. Seeing that it was 5.45, I found this totally ludicrous and left everything I'd bought right there in front of her till and walked off with nothing, telling her to put it all back on the shelves herself. It didn't go down a storm when I got home with absolutely nothing for the kids to eat, but there are times when these things have to be done.

We once had a particularly bloody-minded overnight attendant on our car park at Capital, many years ago. At 5.45 every morning for five years he had said a rather frosty, 'Good morning, Mr Tarrant', and then insisted on checking my identity pass. One morning, I arrived in a panic, late for my breakfast show and without my pass. There was a queue at the barrier which was making me even later, but when I finally got to the front the gentleman told me, with undisguised glee, that I couldn't come in because I didn't have my pass.

'But it's me!' I pleaded. 'You know it's me. It's always been me, every morning for the last five years and I'm supposed to be on the radio in exactly two and a half minutes.'

This revelation made our man even happier, of course,

and he ecstatically replied, 'Sorry – no pass, no entry into this car park.'

At 5.58 on a dark February morning I didn't really feel there was much point pleading any longer as I knew it would only make him even happier. So I got out of my car, locked it up right in front of the barrier, and walked away.

It caused chaos but it made me very, very happy and, five minutes later, an extremely apologetic manager rang on the studio phone to say he was deeply sorry for his man's ridiculous attitude and would I please, please, pretty please send the keys down and he would personally park it for me in my normal bay.

As you can imagine, I'm normally an easy-going enough sort of bloke, as my road rage therapist will tell you, but once in a while we all have to stand up and be counted.

One Saturday evening, just before Christmas a couple of years ago, a particularly bumptious young yuppie was holding up a whole side street in London by parking his brand new bright red Porsche right in the middle of the road. The sickening little brat was strolling up and down the pavement looking for a particular flat and, while cars trying to go in both directions tooted their horns at him furiously, he refused to be hurried and gave us all the 'V' sign. After about the third 'V' sign I have to admit shamefully that I snapped.

I drove my rather larger, heavier car forward and took off the whole side of his pretty little sports car, to a loud cheer from everybody else in the road. It cost me a fortune to pay for his repairs, I lost my no claims bonus and, I

admit, it was a totally irresponsible thing to have done. I also have to tell you that the precise second when my front bumper made contact with his wing, was one of the happiest moments of my life!

Murray Mints

Over the years I must have given away hundreds of thousands of pounds! Before you start jumping to the conclusion that I'm some sort of latter day St Francis of Assisi, I hasten to make it quite clear that none of it was ever my own money. It's always belonged to some hugely rich company like Capital Radio or ITV. I've given away brand new cars, holidays in just about every exotic resort in the world and literally sacks full of money.

I've done all sorts of radio competitions and TV game shows, some of them very ingenious and some of them frankly incomprehensible. I've given people £50,000 just for knowing their birthday. I've given people two weeks in the Seychelles for gargling Christmas carols with their heads in buckets of water. I've given away booby prizes like drawing pins, hairy toffees and even a disgusting old newsreader's vest. I mean that the vest was old and disgusting, not the newsreader. I think.

People taking part in competitions are often very strange. Women are always much better at sounding excited and grateful than the blokes ever are. Even when they win very large cash prizes, men seem to have a real problem sounding genuinely delighted, while the women scream ecstatically at the top of their voices. I've never really understood it, but I think the bottom line is that men are too self-conscious, too worried about losing what they believe to be their dignity and composure in front of a live audience. I think men, to use a technical expression, have got their heads too far up their own arses!

Over the years, I must have talked to thousands of contestants, on all sorts of quizzes. The memory of most of them, I have to admit, is a bit of a blur. But of course there are some that will always stick in my mind.

There was the incredibly brave but clearly potty bloke called Jim from Basildon in Essex who had won £12,000 one morning on a Double Or Quits radio competition. In tax free cash, it was probably as much as he earned in a year. But he then decided, in spite of my pleas and those of all his factory mates in the background, to go ahead and double it on the toss of a coin. Needless to say, Jim lost the lot.

There was another woman who missed out on £20,000 because she believed that the capital of India was Moscow . . .

And my favourite was a girl who had to tell me the name of Britain's best-known motor racing commentator. In a production meeting before the show I remember saying, 'Oh, come on – that's much too easy. Everybody in the country knows it's Murray Walker!'

I was wrong. This girl simply couldn't remember his name. We went through Damon Hill, Emerson Fittipaldi,

Jackie Stewart and even, rather puzzlingly, Ryan Giggs. I was desperately trying to help.

'Give me a few more seconds', she kept saying. 'It's on the tip of my tongue.'

I was running out of ideas for helpful clues. Eventually, I thought of Murray Mints.

'All right,' I said. 'One last chance, on the tip of your tongue – it's something that you suck.'

Without a second's hesitation, she said, 'Oh yes, of course – Dickie Davis.'

First Kiss

As a reporter once working for ATV I had to film a ludicrous event that they hold every year in Santa Fe, 'The Great Non-Stop All Night New Mexico Kissing Party'. It sounded terrific fun and I just assumed it involved rampant couples snogging each other non-stop for hour after hour until they either had to have a bucket of cold water thrown over them to cool their ardour, or be separated with a tyre lever.

But in reality it was nothing like that at all. Far from kissing anybody else, the contestants had to kiss a car . . . Admittedly, it was a very nice car – a brand new 1979 Chevrolet, and the one who could kiss it non-stop for the longest time got to keep it and drive it home – but it was an absolutely potty idea for a competition. It's held every year and huge crowds turn out to cheer on the half crazed contestants as they smooch the hours away with the four wheeled object of their desire.

Most of them actually only lasted half an hour or so, which still seemed to me a very long time to be kissing a Chevrolet's bumper, but by about midnight there were just two women left. And so it went on, and on, and on. Past sunrise, past lunchtime the next day, past supper time, until eventually sometime past 8 p.m. on the second evening, one woman could stand it no longer. She dragged her split and bleeding lips away from her dream machine's bonnet and sobbed uncontrollably. The winner then whooped with delight, fanning the air triumphantly with her fist. She tried to give several of the US TV crews a victorious interview, but was physically incapable of passing anything remotely comprehensible through the bruised remains of her mouth and drove off delightedly in her brand new car, her lips still shaped like a sink plunger. She had kissed that Chevrolet non-stop for just over twenty-six hours!

Driving back to my motel and mulling over the whole extraordinary contest and the events of the last long, dull twenty-four hours, I found myself thinking about what a nasty, unhygienic business kissing is anyway. I still shudder at the memory of my first kiss, even though it was at least a hundred years ago.

I was a little wolf-cub with short trousers, knobbly knees and an irresistible little woggle, and she was a great heaving girl guide called Daphne. We were walking home from our regular Tuesday evening cubs, brownies, guides and scouts night in our local church hall near Reading in

Berkshire when she suddenly grabbed hold of my shoulders, wrenched my head back, almost knocking my cap off, and forced her great sink plunger of a tongue down my throat. I had no idea what she was doing. At first I thought perhaps she was looking for something. I remember being absolutely revolted by the whole business and, many years and six kids later, I still am.

A couple of years ago, this same brazen Daphne appeared on Noel Edmonds's *Telly Addicts*, announcing shamelessly that her main claim to fame was that she gave Chris Tarrant his first kiss.

Noel seemed to find this terribly funny. She seemed to find it terribly funny and I, sitting at home alone, found the whole memory quite horrifying as it slowly came flooding back. Not wearing her girl guide's uniform, Daphne looked altogether different! But then, without my grey shorts and my funny little woggle, so do I.

A Shocking Story

One of the most ridiculous stories I covered in my reporting days concerned the wife who came home to witness her husband being electrocuted. No, that's not the ridiculous bit. The ridiculous bit was what she did next.

'There he was,' she said, 'frantically shaking and vibrating in the kitchen with what looked like a wire running from his waist to the electric kettle.'

In an inspired life-saving bid, she picked up a hefty piece of wood and smashed it with a mighty blow against her husband in an attempt to wrench him off the 240 volt-current surging through his body. In doing so, she shattered his arm in two places.

Her husband, to put it politely, wasn't best pleased. Far from being electrocuted, he was in fact listening to his Walkman and doing a particularly energetic, gyrating disco dance.

His first words, once he'd stopped his agonized screaming, were, 'Now what have I done?'

'Honestly, darling – I was trying to save your life!' she sobbed.

History doesn't relate how he expressed his gratitude.

But if they are still married, I bet he's labelled his Walkman in very big letters.

Sex Survey

If you're one of those quaint old-fashioned things who still thinks of bed as the centre for your lovemaking, boy are you out of date. Or, to be more precise, girl are you out of date!

A caller to my breakfast show one morning gleefully told me the gory details of a survey he'd just been paid to carry out among over 3,000 women about places where they liked to make love.

The girls, as usual, were brutally frank about the whole business and among the more extraordinary places they had made love were in a hearse, in a car boot, in a graveyard, in a dentist's chair, in a gorse bush, on a billiard table, a lawn mower, a garage roof, a fridge, a wall heater, the boss's desk, a franking machine and a fish tank. Most athletic of all were the eleven girls, out of the 3,000 interviewed, who admitted they'd had sex up a tree!

Presumably it's mainly done in the summer – before the fall of the autumn leaves. But in any case, who are these women and, more importantly, where can I find one, and what sort of trees are they? You could do yourself a terrible mischief up a conker tree. Holly is definitely one to avoid, and in these days of fear of all things sexually

transmitted, who needs the added risk of catching Dutch elm disease?

I suppose, if nothing else, the survey revealed the origins of the expression 'a night on the nest' . . .

Finders Keepers

I'm an honest enough sort of bloke . . . if you leave your wallet on the sofa in my house, it'll still be there when you come back for it. Most of the money will have gone and all the credit cards, but the wallet will still be there!

All right, that was a joke. Honestly. But I don't think I would be as honest about unexpected windfalls – with the continuing recession, inflation, income tax, soaring property prices and extortionate bank charges, I think any little strokes of luck should be treated with a strictly 'finders keepers' attitude. Or 'keepers for as long as you can' anyway.

That's why, when I covered her story for the *Sunday Mirror* once, I couldn't for the life of me feel any admiration for someone as honest as forty-year-old Alaide Oliveira who had a bank computer error in her favour. The bank's mistake was to pay £887,000 into her account. Her reaction was to ring them at once and tell them about the error.

I'm sorry, but I think she's raving mad. I would have kept absolutely silent about it and left it there quietly accumulating interest by the day until somebody

somewhere spotted their blunder. Life is hard and then you die, but in the meantime grab these little presents from heaven with both hands!

I'd like to tell you that the bank rewarded Alaide's honesty, but apart from a nice 'thank you' letter from the manager, she got nothing 'because it's not the bank's money'.

Her current account went back to its true balance – of thirty-eight quid.

Well, I'm a Monkey's Uncle

I was guesting on a radio station in the States one week when their special guest of the morning was a scientist – a guy called Professor Stephen Seger – who asked, live on air, for female volunteers to give birth to test tube gorillas!

Only in America would anybody make such a request on the radio and, even more to the point, only in America would five women step forward to give the dreadful sounding business a try.

The experiment was apparently necessary because the rare mountain gorilla is heading for extinction and despite the fact that, at birth, a baby gorilla can weigh up to 15lbs, the women were all very keen and excited at the prospect. Even as a bloke, the whole conversation was making my eyes water, but the girls were positively looking forward to conception, pregnancy and birth. One particularly out-

spoken surrogate mother, an obsessive and very intimidating German animal lover called Sabine, had so far only specialized in giving birth to baby humans, but was desperate to do her bit for the environment and said she could be available to get across to the clinic within the hour.

'My husband probably isn't going to be very happy about it. But who cares what he thinks, let's get it on!' she added.

I understand that several of the couplings of girl and gorilla did actually take place – well, girl and test tube gorilla anyway. But it wasn't a great success and the poor old mountain gorilla is still in deep trouble.

Also in deep trouble is Sabine's marriage. Her husband was even less keen on the idea than she feared he might be and is currently suing her for divorce on the grounds of test tube adultery. I can just imagine the divorce court proceedings

'Who do you cite in zis case?' the German m'Lud would ask.

To which Sabine's husband would say, 'The big hairy one in the corner, peeling a banana with his feet'!

A Good Year for the Noses

A couple of years ago, when all the countries in Europe were squabbling over the complexities of the Maastricht treaty, a particularly bizarre and puzzling example of

international goodwill was suddenly announced in the Far East on our 6.30 a.m. news.

Apparently, the Japanese had agreed to ship 20,000 noses – yes, that's noses – to South Korea in an attempt to improve diplomatic relations between the two countries. It wasn't for some mass convention of the oriental branch of the Barbra Streisand fan club, but in fact a return of the spoils of war. It seems that back in 1597, the Japanese invaded the southern part of Korea, and chopped the noses off everyone they met in battle. Then, for reasons known only to themselves, the Japanese warriors piled these noses up, presumably all shapes and sizes of them, shoved them into boxes, carted them back home to Okayama and buried them in a 'nose tomb'!

I would imagine that the 'nose tomb' didn't figure too highly on the list of attractions tourists to Japan frequently visited so, centuries later, the Japanese decided it might be a nice bit of PR if they shoved all the noses back into boxes and shipped them back to South Korea.

There was a special welcoming committee on the dockside in South Korea when the boat-load of noses arrived. I felt particularly sorry for the poor South Korean official who was given the task of reuniting all 20,000 noses with the descendants of the original owners. A strong press rumour circulated that Michael Jackson was going to make an appearance to rummage through the bunch and take his pick. Unsurprisingly it turned out to be just another hype by the relentless Jackson press machine.

Perhaps it's just me being silly, but I'd have thought a more effective enticement towards the promotion of Far

Eastern goodwill would have been to send great sackloads of money, rather than a mountain of 400-year-old noses, but what do I know . . . or should that be 'nose'?

Taking the Plunge

Never work with children or animals, is the old adage. And it's absolutely true. Over the years my dealings with animals on live TV have included breaking two ribs when I fell off an elephant, being bitten by a python – okay, so they're not poisonous but a snake bite's still a snake bite! – being bitten at the very top of my leg by a ferret and having my fingers stomped on by a rodeo horse.

Silly stories involving kids on TV are endless – but my favourite is the little five-year-old boy who, live on *Tiswas,* wanted to say hello to his teacher.

'Okay,' I said, 'go ahead. What's she called?'

'Mrs Carter,' he replied. 'But we all call her stinky farter.'

So they're right about not working with kids or animals but somebody should also have added 'Don't work with Freddie Starr or eighty-year-old super athletes'!

When I spent a summer working for TV-am out and about on the Great British sea front, it was a splendid four weeks but the schedule was ridiculous. Every night we would arrive in a new seaside town, more or less throw together a show for the next morning, have a few beers, sometimes have a lot of beers, and go to bed. Bear in

mind that, at that time, TV-am's survival, just days after the abrupt exit of the Famous Five, was constantly hanging by a thread.

Each morning just finding that our cameras still hadn't yet been repossessed by the finance company and that there was a large crowd waiting for us on the beach was very gratifying. What the large crowd didn't know was how very thrown together the whole thing was and all items and guests had been booked in a panic only the day before.

In Blackpool we somehow got the Mayoress dancing on the beach in the arms of a man in a gorilla suit, who then caused chaos by goosing one of the dancers. In Scarborough we booked a very nice classical orchestra who even agreed to turn up at 6.15 in the morning in dinner jackets, bow ties, the lot, only to find that half way through their live performance the tide came roaring up Scarborough beach and washed music and musicians away. Mike, our floor manager, had misread the local tide tables and was an hour out. In Brighton, during the final round of a live Miss Lovely Legs competition, an escaped loony, wearing a long mac and carrying a string bag full of plasticine models, appeared from the local funny farm and joined in amongst the parading beauty queens. He was taken away, kindly but firmly, still clutching his shopping and put into a Panda car. In Rhyl, north Wales, the nice locals warned us it could sometimes get a bit rough in the evenings. I'll say it could! As we took a quiet stroll along the high street the night that we arrived, the scene suddenly transformed into something more in keeping

with Dodge City in the days of the Wild West. A large bar stool came flying out through the window of the first pub that we passed, swiftly followed by a fat bloke wearing a blood stained T-shirt.

There was glass everywhere, there was blood everywhere and everybody suddenly seemed to be hitting everybody else. Police cars with flashing sirens came racing to the scene and took offenders away by the barrow load. It was no huge deal in itself, but bearing in mind we'd only been in Rhyl ten minutes, it made us a little wary of what might happen the next morning live on TV.

In actual fact, Rhyl went almost smoothly by TV-am's standards. There was a particularly fine singing dog item, a hypnotist who managed to burn somebody's fingers with his cigarette lighter – a volunteer who clearly wasn't in as deep a trance as the hypnotist had believed – and the whole show closed with a how much do you look like Roland Rat competition. All very exciting stuff and how nice to be on the cutting edge of current affairs first thing in the morning.

Whoever worked out our itinerary clearly hadn't got an atlas, or even a globe, as they'd booked us to arrive in Great Yarmouth that night, which is about as far across the UK from Rhyl as Moscow is from Johannesburg. So we said our fond farewells to the good people of north Wales and raced across Britain towards Norfolk with our researchers on the new-fangled mobile phones as we travelled, trying to set up some sort of a show for the next morning in Yarmouth.

To give the producer and the researchers their due,

they didn't do a bad job at all. They managed to book Freddie Starr, who was appearing in Great Yarmouth's summer season, the local beauty queen, a Punch and Judy person and one of those pillars of society who seems to exist in every seaside town in this country; an old boy who goes swimming in the sea every single day of the year – come rain, hail or snow.

This remarkable old gentleman was eighty-four years old, brown as a berry and had swum in the sea off Great Yarmouth every day, including Christmas Day, for over forty years, or something like that. So the show sounded particularly promising, admittedly by our rather easily-pleased standards.

Next day I said good morning to Nick Owen and Anne Diamond back in the studio, the big crowd that had already turned up at half past six on the Great Yarmouth sea front gave a big cheer and Freddie Starr ran around goosing the over-forties aerobics dancers who were trying to follow the manic instructions of mad Lizzie, our resident keep fit fanatic. It was all good, silly fun and going worryingly well until the point that I cued the eighty-four-year-old swimmer to dive into the north sea.

I had to say the magic words, 'And now, racing down the beach beside me here at Yarmouth, is a remarkable old super fit octogenarian who's plunged into the sea at this point every day for the last forty-three years.'

The remarkable old gentleman got his cue and off he went towards the sea. Unfortunately, in our conversations with him, all done hurriedly on the phone the day before, nobody had checked out whether he'd got both legs. So,

suddenly, at 6.35 on a mid-summer's morning, the whole of Britain was treated to the extraordinary sight of a demented-looking one-legged man hopping down the beach as best he could with just an unmistakable flap of skin showing out of the other empty swimming trunk leg as he bounced towards the waves. It was made extra disturbing for the viewers, who were just about settling down to their breakfast, by the cameraman going in for a great big close-up of the one leg protruding from the ocean, as he made his glorious dive.

I shamefacedly admit the crew and I had nervous hysterics on the spot, the crowd went into a shocked silence and Freddie Starr roared past me pretending to be Hitler, but with only one leg, and stuck his tongue in my ear.

The director hurriedly cut back to Nick and Anne in the studio who were sitting looking gobsmacked at the pictures coming up from Great Yarmouth. The switchboard was predictably jammed with complaints about 'Typical tasteless Tarrant and Starr behaviour', 'Sick idea of a joke', etc.

I have to say, in fairness to myself and Freddie, it was a genuine mistake because nobody had actually met the man before the morning of the show and hadn't even seen him changed into his swimming costume until seconds before he was cued, so nobody had any idea of his disability.

But, if nothing else, the whole episode did contribute yet one more golden rule to the trainee TV researchers' guidebook of how to stay in work. From then on, every single conversation I overheard from the guys in the background fixing up items and guests for the rest of the summer shows would begin like this:

'Hello – it's TV-am here and our outside broadcast cameras will be in your area tomorrow morning. Now, before we go any further, I know it sounds like a silly question, but have you got both your legs?'

Commentary in Sound Only

Here's another lesson learnt the hard way; one that once it has happened in your TV career, you'll never, ever forget.

COMMENTARY IN SOUND ONLY

In the mid seventies, I was briefed to do a light-hearted report for ATV on how the atmosphere among the crowds at cricket matches had changed. Until just a few years earlier, spectators at English cricket grounds might as well not have been there for all the players and umpires knew. While crowds in Australia, India and the Caribbean were known for their loud exuberance, the much more reserved English had traditionally maintained a stiff upper lip and virtual silence throughout all but the most exciting matches. At most, there would be a polite ripple of applause when someone like Peter May or Ted Dexter scored a century after two days undefeated batting, or there might be a murmur of 'Good shot' when a six was sweetly struck out of the ground. But in the main, it was frowned on to make any sort of noise during a match.

It was the very essence of Englishness, and any other sort of behaviour was, well, simply not cricket. However, the arrival of some of the brilliant teams from the Caribbean in the seventies, when the West Indies produced probably the most exciting and successful cricketers of all time in front of their whooping adoring fans who'd come to live in England, changed all that. The crowds were tremendous and around the same time one-day Sunday cricket matches were introduced in this country for the very first time.

One-day games tend to be much more dramatic, and have to be completed in the one day, come what may. The combination of the one-day league and the visiting West Indians completely changed the atmosphere inside the cricket grounds of England.

Of course this horrified the establishment, particularly at Lord's which remains in its own little time warp to this very day, but loud wildly cheering crowds became common place.

For my TV report we dug out some great old footage of the scene at Edgbaston cricket ground in the fifties, with almost the whole crowd fast asleep during a particularly dull five-day test match, and compared it with recent scenes from the Warwickshire ground when there had been a pitch invasion to greet a quite breathtaking century scored in double quick time by the legendary Garfield Sobers.

'In just a few years there's been an incredible change,' I reported. 'At grounds like Edgbaston, where just a few years ago the crowd remained virtually silent throughout the day, they now sing and dance and beat steel drums throughout the match in a marvellous non-stop carnival atmosphere.

'Of course,' I went on, 'it does occasionally get a bit too much. Cans of Red Stripe beer have been known to be thrown at fielders close to the boundary and abuse has been shouted at umpires, using the sort of vocabulary normally only saved for referees at football matches.'

Because this was a pre-recorded item the producer and I agreed we'd put a few strategic bleeps over my report at the point where I described the actual sort of language the crowd shouted at umpires.

So I said, 'You know the sort of vocabulary: "What's the matter with you, umpire, are you completely blooming

blind? You need to buy a pair of glasses you silly blinking idiot. You're a total dashed rotter . . .'''

I recorded it exactly like that. We put the bleeps over words like blooming and blinking and watched it played back in the control room. But somehow it just didn't quite work. Although you couldn't hear what words I was saying under the bleeps, you could just tell, somehow, that I wasn't using *the* words. I didn't look authentic, it looked plain daft.

'No problem,' said the producer. 'We'll record it again, Chris, and this time you can use *the* words. We'll still bleep it carefully, of course, but this way, it'll look spot on.'

I needed no second bidding, of course, and safe in the knowledge that it was all going to be covered over with bleeps I told the cameras exactly what the crowd thought of the umpire, with several fs, a couple of bs and even a 'w'! It was great fun. The crew and I really enjoyed it. The producer had a field day in the editing room with the bleep effects, and we all agreed it was now exactly right. You couldn't hear the rude words but it looked absolutely authentic which, of course, it was. The item went out on the *Six O'clock Show* that night. All the bleeps were in the right places and the producer, the crew and I all agreed that it was a really good item.

Only – and here's why I said at the outset that there are lessons in TV that once you've learnt them you never, ever forget them – as soon as the item had gone out the phones started ringing and ringing and ringing as hundreds of absolutely outraged deaf people rang in to complain!

The Dying Fly

Jasper had an idea. Being Carrott, he had lots of ideas. And in those days before he became the world's richest human being, he used to tell them to us a lot in the *Tiswas* production office. Some of them were very funny, some of them were extremely unfunny and downright daft.

'Let's all do the Dying Fly, and get all the kids doing it as well,' he said.

'Great,' we said. 'Brilliant. Just what we need – er . . . by the way . . . what the hell is it?'

'The Dying Fly. You must know the Dying Fly. Sometimes it's called dead ants. You must know it – it's, well, you sort of get your legs in the air and sort of . . . oh, sod it, I'll show you . . .'

So there and then, in our production office – all right, actually it was an Indian restaurant in Birmingham – Carrott solemnly moved a few plates and knives and forks, lay on his back on our table and started kicking his little legs and arms in the air like a loony looking for his lost bicycle.

'Course, you'd be wearing antennae stuck on your heads,' he said helpfully. 'And there'd be some music.'

'Yes, er, of course,' we mumbled.

Apparently Carrott had been doing a concert in Gates-

head that hadn't gone down a storm and, at the end, as he was saying goodnight and desperately looking round the room for the fire exit, this enormous Geordie got up on the stage saying 'Why aye man' and 'Real bootta for tea'. Then he asked: 'Aren't you going to do the Dyin' Fly?'

'Er, yes,' replied a bewildered Carrott, just wanting to get out alive. 'You start it off and we'll all do it whenever you like pal . . .'

So this huge oak tree gets down on his back on the stage and starts kicking his arms and legs in the air, followed by the whole audience and, finally, a thoroughly confused Carrott.

Jasper left the theatre to a standing ovation.

'What an entertainer, comic genius man, why aye, great man, let's go and sink a few Newcastle Browns, real bootta . . .'

Sure enough there we all were the next Saturday lying on our backs in studio three with little antennae on our heads, kicking our arms and legs like loonies to a catchy little tune called the typewriter song.

The thing became a cult. All over the country the music would start up and people would get down on their backs and do the Dying Fly. There were all-night Dying Fly marathons, attempts on the 'how many people can we get doing the Dying Fly all at once in one place' world record. We even made a disc – selling literally dozens of copies.

I was asked along to a fancy dress party at a ladies' college once and halfway through the evening the sight of all these eighteen-year-olds dressed mainly in St Trinian's gear, gym slips and stocking tops, all getting down on their backs and kicking their legs in the air for two minutes and forty eight seconds is a sight I'll never forget – nor ever try to.

It all ended rather abruptly. People started doing the Dying Fly in the daftest places, like dual carriageways. It sounds ridiculous now, but that really is what happened. There were several near misses and finally a really serious accident and we were forced to abandon it before the Dying Fly actually did kill somebody.

Every few months ROSPA used to publish a list of the 'things most likely to cause accidents' and at the end of 1978 I received a very official-looking bit of paper that read something like this:

Top ten most dangerous practices for last quarter, ending 30 November:

Drunken driving	Storing petrol
Excessive speed	Weed killers
Poor car mechanics	DYING FLY
No crash helmet	Faulty wiring
Fireworks	Unlicensed explosives.

This Is Your Life

I always said I'd avoid *This Is Your Life* like the proverbial plague, and that anyone with even half a brain would see the big red book coming a mile off. Well, I'm here to tell you that it doesn't work like that.

The moment when the hapless individual is confronted by Michael Aspel and 'the book' is referred to by the production team as 'the hit' and they refer to you as 'the subject'. This I discovered with the benefit of hindsight, having been repeatedly referred to as 'the subject' by my driver on the way to 'the hit' as he was on the phone making sure that events proceeded smoothly. All 'subjects' have a code name – apparently mine was 'city' (for CT); Trevor Macdonald was 'burger' and Robert Maxwell was 'house' – presumably because he was the size of one!

When they got me, I was doing a simple handover, or so I thought, of a minibus to a handicapped kids' school called the Phoenix Centre down in Kent. I'd done my breakfast show in the morning and more or less went straight there. What I didn't realize was that all my mates

at Capital, Ingrid my wife, all my kids, my mother, my father and dozens of other people I hadn't seen for twenty or thirty years had all been making frantic secret phone calls to each other for over a month.

As I officially handed over the minibus, I remember thinking, 'Why is that silly ambulance getting in the way at just the wrong moment', when the doors of said silly ambulance opened and Michael Aspel came flying out, clutching the famous red book.

It was one of the most unforgettable moments of my life. It just doesn't occur to you that it will ever really happen, or that it could possibly happen without you getting a hint of it. In the event I had not a clue – I was like a lamb to the slaughter.

Once I got over the initial shock and was raced across to Teddington studios, the show itself was an absolute hoot. All sorts of old mates from way back when came on: a completely mad teacher called 'Maeve the Rave' appeared and told about the days when I lived outside the school in the mini van; all my old mates from *Tiswas* came on and talked about what I did while the cartoons were on; Mike Rutherford and Phil Collins from *Genesis* talked about the days when I stuffed the two of them into giant flowerpots and covered them in custard; Lenny Henry talked about how difficult it was for a black guy with short curly hair to be a head banger; Jeremy Beadle came on and took his trousers off for no reason that anybody ever really understood; and my little boy Toby, who was only just five, suddenly appeared on film from his bed, explaining that he couldn't be with daddy because

that very morning he'd developed chickenpox – or, as he calls them, 'chickenpops'.

It was a brilliant atmosphere and silliest of all was Jasper Carrot who came on to remind us of the days when he taught us all to do the Dying Fly.

The whole fiasco ended with all of us, celebrities, uncles, aunties and all, and even the normally super-smooth Michael Aspel, lying on our backs on the studio floor, waving our arms and kicking our legs in the air. It was a ridiculous show, but once I was over the initial shock I have to admit that I enjoyed it hugely.

The build up to the 'hit' is real soap opera stuff. Everyone contacted is warned on pain of death to keep the whole thing totally secret. And if it ever does get out the show has to be cancelled, even at the very last minute, and the team start all over again on somebody else. Such cancellations are a huge disappointment for everyone involved, a massive waste of everybody's time and, of course, hugely expensive.

There have been a number of memorable situations over the years – Danny Blanchflower, the Irish international footballer, was the first person ever to refuse point blank to do the show. He left Eamonn Andrews and the crew standing there with their mouths opening and closing like goldfish. Mercifully it's only happened a couple of times since, which is not bad at all for a show that's run for over forty years. Everybody says they'd walk out, but of course they never do. Richard Gordon, the author of *Doctor in the House*, nearly did! In the days when the show used to be live on air, he said, 'Oh balls' and walked off. Eventually he calmed down and was talked into it by frantic producers.

But there have been all sorts of problems – David Walker, the manager of my old mates *Status Quo*, pulled the band out of the show at the very last minute, causing chaos to Thames Television, because with their number of ex-wives, step kids, etc., it was just getting too complicated and too close to the bone to be worth risking.

In their manager's words, 'We're a very successful band, we just don't need the grief.'

The late Les Dawson very nearly got divorced over the show. Time and again Les would come home late at night, to find his wife suddenly putting the phone down and looking embarrassed as he walked in. She even began sleeping in the spare room because she was terrified of talking about the show in her sleep. Soon Les was convinced that dear Meg was having an affair. Of course she wasn't, but it was only after the show that she could tell him what had been happening.

Ronnie Barker also became convinced that his wife was being unfaithful. It didn't help matters when one of the young researchers on the show left her his card and Ronnie found it. It was impossible for Mrs Barker to explain what her relationship with this man was, so Ronnie rang the number and a man answered the phone saying 'Hello, *This Is Your Life*! How can I help you?' The secret was out and the show had to be cancelled.

Incidentally, the production team were told, from that day on, never, ever to answer the phone with the words '*This Is Your Life*' again!

Colin Milburn, the brilliant England and Northampton batsman, is probably the only person ever to appear in the opening credits of *This Is Your Life* and then never actually be seen on the show itself. The subject of the show was the late, brilliant Willie Rushton. Myself, Colin Milburn, Michael Parkinson, Nicholas Parsons and a load of other cricketing Lord's Taverners were taken up to the front of a pub on the open top of a horse drawn carriage to take the focus away from the then presenter Eamonn Andrews, who was hiding in amongst us all with a blanket over his head, clutching the red book. It was a cold afternoon and there were a couple of very handy little hip flasks being handed around while we waited. Milburn had come on the train from Newcastle, had had a few bevvies on the way down so that by the time we got to Eamonn's big moment, Mr Milburn, like Jeffrey Barnard, was distinctly unwell. In fact, by this time, Colin was as unwell as a newt. And, even worse, the 'hit' on Rushton was going to be done in a pub that had stayed open especially all afternoon.

They cued the cameras, we bounced along happily behind the horses, with Milburn still sneaking the occasional nip from the life-saving hip flask and Eamonn sprang out on the unsuspecting Rushton. I say unsuspecting, but Willie was the most calm and unfazed subject that I've ever seen on the show.

When Eamonn appeared maniacally screaming, 'This is your life!', Willie just said, 'Oh, there you are you funny little leprechaun – I've been waiting for you for years.'

We piled into the pub and Milburn bought an enormous round of drinks, then proceeded to fall fast asleep in the corner of the bar. We pushed him into a taxi and made our way to the Thames Studios, where the big man woke up just enough to drink half a bottle of wine before sitting as best he could on his seat in among the Taverners in the studio. By now big Colin was absolutely paralytic and feeling no pain whatsoever. After several fruitless calls for quiet from the floor manager so that we could start the show, the amiable but incomprehensible Colin was asked if he wouldn't mind leaving. It was all perfectly polite and hassle free. Slurring the words 'I'm terribly sorry but I really don't feel so great', he was quietly put into a car, helped back on to the train and was back in Newcastle before the pubs shut. Willie Rushton wrote him a very nice thank you letter for coming along to pay tribute and I don't think Colin ever realized that he never actually quite made it to the show itself.

One person who always seems to make it to the show is Frank Carson. He seems to have popped up somehow, welcome or not, in the life of just about every man and woman in the country. He's always available, or makes himself available, he's always popular and he's always got something funny to say about everybody. He's probably been on the show more than anyone else in Britain – probably even more than Michael Aspel or Eamonn Andrews.

At one stage he was on show after show during a particular series. It had become so ridiculous that he used to

sign off with, 'That's it from me, big Frank – Eamonn, I'll see you next week!'

It also became a running joke that Frank himself had never been the programme's subject – always the bridesmaid, never the bride! It was probably because none of the other guests would have a chance to get a word in edgeways. But although he and Eamonn both lived in Dublin, and they would see each other regularly on the planes to and from London, Frank himself was never the 'life'. Every time Frank saw Eamonn, Frank would pretend to run off, saying, 'You'll never get me. I know you've got the red book in that briefcase.' But, of course, Eamonn hadn't.

This went on for several years, and then one day Eamonn was flying across to Heathrow from Dublin and Frank came and sat next to him on the plane. For the umpteenth time, Carson started going through his usual routine, with Eamonn saying, as usual, 'Don't be so silly, Frank – we've got loads of much bigger stars lined up for the next five years', when all of a sudden, as they were leaving the aircraft, a film crew appeared out of nowhere and Eamonn produced the red book from under a coat that he'd had on his knee all the way across the Irish sea. On the front were the legendary words 'This is your life – Frank Carson' and Frank, for once, and probably for the only time in his life, was absolutely gobsmacked. The silence lasted for nearly two whole seconds!

The Cage

At the height of *Tiswas* fame in the late seventies, 58% of the audience were over sixteen. Pubs opened early on Saturday mornings with giant TVs over the bar. It was obligatory viewing on all the sets in TV hire shops and it was certainly on in every student union in the country, which I found a bit of a worry even at the time and, having met many of today's captains of industry and members of parliament, it seems my fears were more than justified!

In some ways, this adult cult following was very gratifying but in many others it made life difficult. With my producer's hat on I was never quite sure what audience we were aiming at. In the end we copped out and just did whatever made *us* laugh and since we were mentally mostly big overgrown kids anyway, it seemed to work quite well. But I was constantly trying to come up with ideas that would somehow cut across all the age groups, and the best idea of all was 'the cage'.

In spite of the fact that it was supposedly a kids' show, we were forever getting requests from people who really should have been old enough to have more sense to come in and sit amongst all the jammy faced kids in the studio. We must have turned down thousands until we hit upon the idea of allowing grown ups in, but keeping them in a holding pen to the side of the action and very close to where we kept all the buckets. If there was a lull in the proceedings – and some Saturdays the lull lasted the full

three hours – we could pelt the grown ups with anything we could lay our hands on.

Admittedly, it was a rather simplistic idea and we intended to try it for one week only. In reality, it ran for more than five years.

All we told the adults the first week was that they had been chosen to join a small selection of lucky mums and dads who would be allowed onto the studio floor during the transmission of the next week's programme. They would be ushered into a private viewing area and they should bring a change of clothes.

The next Saturday, after about five minutes of the programme, Bob Carolgees and I got rather fed up with their grinning simpletons' faces peering at us through the bars of the cage, so we pelted them with the contents of every bucket we could lay our hands on. There was uproar. The kids went wild with delight at the vision of their mothers and fathers completely coated in green gunge. The adults screamed in horrified disbelief and the more they screamed, the more we pelted them. Most ridiculous of all, the grown ups appeared to absolutely love it.

To this day, I have no idea what bizarre raw nerve we touched on, but its effect was instant and massive. On Monday morning the office was besieged with phone calls from supposedly intelligent adults who all wanted to come into the cage and get 'the treatment'. It's presumably something to do with Warhol's theory of everybody wanting their fifteen minutes of fame – but it seemed a funny sort of fame to me. By the Wednesday, we had a waiting list for the cage to last us the whole series. By the next

Friday we had a waiting list of big soft nellies that would have lasted us the rest of our lives.

So the cage became a fixture. Each week a dozen or so lucky, lucky adults would arrive like lambs to the slaughter. It always amused me that despite knowing what to expect many of them would arrived dressed up to the nines – blokes in their best suits, women in specially purchased new dresses and immaculate hair dos, only to be splattered beyond recognition, often within seconds of the opening titles. One women told me she later watched the whole show on video and even she couldn't work out which one she was.

Early every Saturday morning, the lads in the props crew would be busily filling up the gunge buckets ready for that morning's cage-dwellers – mainly water and green and yellow foam, although they told me they also made up extra buckets that they called their 'little specials'. They never would tell me what the ingredients of their little specials were, but I had a few nasty ideas.

After a while we began to advertise for rather specialized cage occupants, usually restricted to the absolute pillars of society – headmasters, maths teachers and the like – just the sort of figures of authority that kids wanted to see get their come-uppance Tiswas cage style! We soon extended our criteria to the sort of strata of society that we wanted to see get their come-uppance, and still there was no shortage of volunteers. We had whole cages full of tax inspectors, traffic wardens, policemen, bank managers, VAT men, solicitors, MPs, even (oh joy!) estate agents. The waiting list grew

and grew and the props men happily prepared their 'little specials'!

One week, in a moment of madness, I decided we'd get together a celebrity cage. It seemed a good idea at the time – on reflection it was one of the daftest things I've ever done.

We had loads of mates from the music industry who were dying to come in the cage. *Quo*, of course, *Rainbow*, Cozy Powell & Co, Lemmy and *Motorhead*, a couple of the *Pretenders* and an all-girl rock band called *Goldie and the Gingerbreads*. We crammed them all into a special extra large cage, added a few pop journalists to the mix and topped it up with John Peel, who was on Radio One then, as indeed he has been for most of this century.

It was a memorable morning. They got an extra special celebrity soaking, of course, but the ad libs were flying all over the place and the atmosphere was tremendous.

About an hour into the show I was in the middle of a sketch with Lenny Henry dressed up as David Bellamy, and a couple of pop stars in ill-fitting, obscene-looking green leotards dressed up as giant sunflowers. All of a sudden the unmistakable smell of marijuana came into my nostrils from the direction of the cage.

Here's me, the producer of a supposed children's television programme – kids everywhere, parents everywhere, journalists everywhere – and one of my guests is smoking a joint!

I abandoned the sketch, to Lenny's bewilderment, and rushed to the cage, completely drenching everyone in it with bucket after bucket of the Midland water board's finest. The offending aroma disappeared. Even now, none of them will tell me who it was smoking pot in the cage that morning – but I've got a pretty good idea. Rock 'n' roll, man – but you try explaining that to the IBA!

Your Future's in the Stars

I've never, ever seen the point of horoscopes. I've never understood them and I've certainly never believed in them. They've always seemed to me to be total mumbo jumbo. Of course I can understand that people need something to believe in, particularly as we get older and more cynical. As we walk through the minefield of life we realize that there are probably only a handful of men and women that we can really trust – but why on earth would one of them be Russell Grant?

People become quite obsessive with horoscopes, letting the ridiculous things completely run their lives, absurdly and blindly believing that the stars control their every action, every waking minute of their day. You know the sort of thing. You're having a dinner party and you get a bit argumentative with someone and they say, 'Ah, of course, you're only saying that because you're a Pisces.'

'No,' I'm thinking, 'I'm only saying that because I've had a skinful of brandy and I want to be stroppy. It's nothing whatsoever to do with my star sign.'

Or there's a girl in the office you fancy rotten, but she

says, 'It would never work because I'm a Sagittarius and you're a Libra.'

And you can't help but think, 'No – it would never really work because I'm married with six kids. My being a Libra is the very least of our problems.'

The heart of the matter is, how can so many absurdly different people all have the same star sign and have anything like a similar behavioural pattern?

Libra is the sign of balance and sensitivity and I share it with, among others, Margaret Thatcher, Martina Navratilova and Edwina Currie. Now I really don't want to have the same sort of day tomorrow as Edwina Currie and I certainly don't want to have the same sort of day as Martina Navratilova!

Others who share the same sign as me include Bill Wyman and Cliff Richard (well they're very similar people, aren't they?); Bob Hoskins, Jimmy Saville, Charles Dance and John Lennon (an unlikely quartet); and the most unlikely pairing of all, Mahatma Ghandi and Hitler's vicious henchman Heinrich Himmler. I think the chances of us all behaving in the same way or reacting in the same way to a similar set of circumstances are absolutely nil. And as for all of us behaving in a typical Libran way, I'm not convinced there was anything particularly balanced about an infamous Nazi mass murderer, was there?

Then there are the people who have an obsessive, if misguided, belief in the secret powers of certain chosen individuals. Probably the all time silliest example of this has her own weekly spot on BBC television. Every Saturday night an audience of around fifteen million people

hang on her every word, however incomprehensible that word might be. Her name is Mystic Meg and she is supposed to be gifted with infinite psychic powers that can see the identity of the National Lottery winner each week.

Yet it is always a great puzzle to me that, if she has such extraordinary powers, why didn't she see the numbers coming up in advance for the very first week of the Lottery, buy the winning ticket and disappear to the Bahamas with ten million quid? I suppose that would be too simple.

Mystic Meg seems the most extraordinary creature to me and the most unlikely booking. Dark, mysterious and undead – and that's only her wig! I know witches keep dead black cats, but they're not supposed to wear them on their head, are they? And I will never understand why the set always looks to be on fire when the cameras come to her. As she sits there in a cloud of dry ice, it's more like a scene from *London's Burning* than an astrological interlude. I've never had a clue what that's all about. Does she have a crafty puff on a pipe to calm her nerves just before her big psychic moment? Or is it just supposed to add to her aura of dark sensuality? If personal magnetism is the intended effect it's certainly wasted on me.

I don't know if the BBC know that we know, but the whole country sussed it very early on as just another way of fleshing out the Lottery programme, which is basically a one minute show. All I want is someone to tell me the winning numbers and to quickly be able to check them.

'Oh, sod it. One out of six – not a bonus ball in sight – back to work on Monday. Still, now we know, we can

all go back down the pub for what remains of Saturday night.'

I don't want jugglers. I don't want fire-eaters. I don't want the new single from someone who was once in *Curiosity Killed the Cat.* I don't want Dale Winton running about dressed up like something out of *Abba.* And I certainly don't want Mystic Meg. I try to analyse what she's talking about each week but every time I come away none the wiser, my TV set gibbering.

'I see a man . . . a tall man . . . and I see the colour red.'

At this point the audience goes absolutely wild with excitement, and on the Monday we read in our morning tabloids that a short woman, three foot six inches high wearing a bright green frock has won £10 million on Saturday night!

No one ever says, 'Let's have a look back to Saturday's show and see how uncannily close Mystic Meg was to foreseeing our winner.'

Of course they don't. Uncannily close? More like absolutely nowhere near.

It may be that about once every three months, a man of slightly above average height wearing a vaguely reddish jumper is one of the 5,000 people who win the consolation prize of a tenner, but my goldfish could guess that right once in a while, according to the laws of probability – and he's been dead for three years!

I once went to see a live clairvoyant show at a theatre in Sussex. There were about 500 people in the audience, and the bloke on stage was having a bit of a hard night of it.

In a hushed voice he said, 'I see a man . . . a man with the name of Dave.'

Everybody looked round – no, nothing.

'Perhaps not Dave,' the clairvoyant continued. 'It might be William.'

Again, absolutely nothing.

And then he said, 'I see a cat.'

A little old lady at the very front put her hand up and said, 'Er, actually, I've got two cats', and the whole audience jumped to their feet and gave him a standing ovation.

WWF Wrestling

My normally very bright, somewhat cynical kids have become obsessed with the totally mindless world of American wrestling. They have turned into total morons and sit glued to this ranting drivel for hours at a time. The constant background soundtrack in my house is of a demented American crowd baying for blood and hysterical American commentators screaming in what might as well be Martian.

When wrestling first appeared on British TV screens in the early seventies, I remember I used to quite enjoy watching it on the telly. Back then they were nice, sensible British wrestlers with nice, sensible British names like 'Mick Mcmanus', 'Jackie Pallou' and 'Big Daddy' – although it was a bit of a shock to discover that Big Daddy's real name was Shirley Crabtree. But this Ameri-

can lot have got names like 'Bam Bam Bigalow', 'Bad News Brown', 'The Undertaker', 'Brett "Hit Man" Heart' and 'Psycho Sid'. There's a bloke called 'Rowdy Roddy Piper' who comes into the ring in a kilt. Now, you'd think any normal person would feel a bit vulnerable in a wrestling ring dressed only in a kilt but it doesn't appear to faze Rowdy Roddy. However, it does help his cause that he also carries bagpipes, which he wraps around his opponents' necks, night after night, sometimes piping almost tunefully while his enemy is slowly garrotted.

The Americans appear to have a rather relaxed attitude to the rules in their wrestling rings. There's a bloke called 'Big Boss Man' who comes in and carries a full size, heavy duty, American policeman's night stick and 'Jake the Snake', who enters carrying a python, which he then gets to bite his opponents, frequently drawing blood!

Presumably nowhere in the small print of the rules

does it say 'Competitors must not bring snakes into the ring', which is a bit of a major oversight. A live snake has got to give you a bit of an edge, surely? I think if I was allowed to take in a king cobra, I'd quite fancy my chances against Evander Holyfield.

I saw one match where a guy hit his opponent repeatedly over the head with a typewriter he'd nicked from the press table, and another where a very long haired opponent suddenly had his hair set on fire by a lighter that his enemy had smuggled into the ring inside his trunks.

They have moves with terrifying names like 'The Pearl River Plunge', 'The Sudden Death Slam' and 'The Gorilla Press', which consists of splitting your opponent's head open with a full size table, which is handily passed under the ropes into the ring at a convenient moment. In one fight I watched, 'Hulk Hogan' had a complete steel cage put around the wrestling ring to stop a particularly cowardly opponent from being able to run away!

The other thing you notice as a spectator is that, in the main, the wrestlers are not the most athletic cross-section of magnificent manhood. In fact a large percentage of them are total porkers.

I was once in Atlanta in one of those 'eat-as-much-as-you-can-for-five-dollars' restaurants, and one particular family – a very large fat man, a much larger, even fatter wife and two obese blobs who were being passed off as kids – were going back and forth to the buffet time and time again. When they got to the dessert they went completely wild, each having at least six or seven different

gooey concoctions, all laced with thick cream and swilling in maple syrup. I lost count of the number of trips made.

I didn't think any more about them until the next morning when I saw the unmistakable blubbery face of the father of the family on a poster outside the main sports stadium in town. He was wrestling that night under the name of 'The Incredible Bulk'!

Several of the American wrestlers look more like Luciano Pavarotti than serious athletes. One guy, who's regularly on the TV over there, is carried in by about eight blokes and placed on an enormous throne. He weighs nearly 600lbs – that's something like forty stones – and wrestles under the name of 'Mabel'.

Enjoy!

Of course it's only a personal thing, but vegetarians are a great worry to me. They always look so pale and usually have to take loads of pills to supplement their diet. They're taking those pills because things are missing in their diet – and what's missing in their diet is a decent steak and kidney pudding. You see them in restaurants trying to look really contented and enthusiastic about two sprigs of lettuce and a rather thin slice of carrot, when I'm sure they're really thinking, 'God, but I fancy that bloke's pork chop.'

It all seems very unbalanced and rather unfair these days – a lots of restaurants now have special vegetarian

menus, but how many vegetarian restaurants have a special menu for meat eaters?

And the stuff they eat! A girl I used to work with was an obsessive veggie, and she'd come back from lunch saying, in all seriousness, that she'd had a really exciting beetroot. Now, I'm sorry, but there is nothing remotely exciting, or ever likely to be, about a beetroot. Even beetroots are bored by other beetroots. And I shudder at the thought of ordering nut cutlets – what man is going to order a dish that sounds like a vasectomy?

Statistically it does appear to be very much a male/female thing. One in ten women is vegetarian but only one in a hundred men. This is probably why so many men are so very fat – but we're happy with it.

You see, in the great scheme of things, we are the hunters, we are natural carnivores! In caveman times, the male was out hunting while the wife was sitting at homing munching on a few leaves thinking, 'I hope to God the silly old fool brings home a decent sized sabre toothed tiger tonight, I'm starving.'

She wouldn't be sitting there thinking, 'I hope he brings home a nice lettuce', would she? Or, 'I hope he manages to club to death a really exciting beetroot'!

And there are no vegetarians in the Bible either, are there? When the Prodigal Son came home, they didn't go out and kill the fatted cabbage, did they? I rest my case.

Last Christmas, my mate Howard Hughes, who reads the early morning news with me on Capital Radio, had his first Christmas Day with his brand new bride. They've

got no kids yet, no relatives were coming round – I was rather envious and the whole thing sounded absolutely perfect. The only problem was that his new bride was vegetarian and Howard was certainly not, so he ordered and ate the whole of an 18lb turkey as she sat there with a spray of millet. Presumably Howard was still eating turkey in the middle of August.

But, gastronomically speaking, my pet hate is nouvelle cuisine. I'm a simple soul – I believe if you pay a large amount of money in a restaurant it would only be fair to have a large amount of food in return. The nouvelle cuisine philosophy seems to be that the more you pay, the less you get! In my dad's day it was called rationing. I always want to go into the kitchen afterwards and give the chef a mouthful – because that's all he's given me. The washing up after five courses can be done in an egg cup and the kitchen staff never have to put any rubbish out because there are never any leftovers. They always give you a great big plate, when they could actually serve the whole thing on a Ritz cracker. It's usually brought in proudly with one of those great big silver lids over the top. Then they stand back, saying, 'Enjoy, enjoy'. I always find myself staring in disbelief, saying, 'Find, find'. Instinctively, I stick my head up underneath the lid to see if perhaps my meal is stuck to the inside, but sadly there's never anything there.

It's always something like two raw spinach leaves in the shape of a leaping gazelle, a tomato carved to look like a rose and a turnip in the shape of a swan. If I want something in the shape of a swan, I want a whole roast

swan please, not a sliver of bloody turnip! And they always bring one of those huge black pepper mills to completely swamp your food – although I suppose that in fairness, when things are really desperate, you can always fill up on the pepper!

Something I have taken to doing, which brings me a perverse amount of happiness, is to wait until the waiter has turned away and retreated about a metre, then call out 'Finished!' at the top of my voice.

The devotees of nouvelle cuisine always insist on the motto 'you eat with your eyes'. I think you probably have to, because there's not much going into your stomach. You may eat with your eyes but you most certainly pay with your credit card!

Slippers Like Kippers

Because I'm a fanatical fisherman, my friends and family always seem to think that any present they give me for my birthday or Christmas is going to be fine by me as long as somehow, somewhere, it's got a fish on it.

They won't buy any actual fishing tackle – partly because they're all too mean – but mainly it's because they reckon that the gear I use is a bit too specialized and they're bound to get me the wrong thing. And in fairness, this is probably true. Buying fishing tackle as a prezzie is bound to be disastrous.

I remember at the age of twenty-eight some well meaning auntie buying me one of those little boy's first fishing kits from Woolworths with a float that even jaws couldn't pull under, an absurdly thick line that could have anchored the Isle of Wight ferry, and with the fishing rod itself made in a quite hideous bright fluorescent pink. Of course, I thanked my auntie profusely and then quietly bunged it on to my local rubbish tip. I couldn't possibly have sat among my mates, who had all the latest, all singing, all dancing gear with that funny little pink thing in my hand could I? Well I could have done but it would almost certainly have led to all sorts of misunderstandings.

So, family and friends have all slowly been educated not even to attempt to buy proper fishing gear for me. Instead, the attitude seems to be that anything else is fine,

as long as there's some vague fish connection somewhere, however tenuous or hideous. I want to take this opportunity in print to tell them that this is not the case!

I'm sure many of my relatives will be absolutely horrified because they've been giving me these things for years and years not knowing how much I hated them all the time. But enough is enough – I really don't want them, I never ever wanted them – and if you trot out the old cliché about me being difficult to buy for, well uncles and aunties everywhere, please try harder!

I can just about stand the odd fishing T-shirt, or even the huge jumper with a great big diving whale on the front that one of my aunts knitted me (it was quite nice actually, although when wearing it I was always terrified of being boarded by Greenpeace), but some of the other 'novelty' ideas have been unbelievable.

For example, you know those hats with knives that go through them? Well, I've had one of those with a trout going through it. Oh, what a laugh. Where on earth was I suppose to wear that? I've had a furry herring to hang off the rear view mirror of my car. I've had fish shaped soap on a rope. I've had a knitted herring shaped toilet roll holder. I've had a block of shaving soap in the shape of a halibut and probably worst of all, I've had a pair of fish-shaped slippers. I'm sorry, and I'm sure they were very well intentioned, but would you want to answer the front door wearing a pair of pilchards?

Master Chef

My cooking is no great shakes. I can just about cook for my own simple needs and without setting light even to the hairs on my legs. I don't blow myself up very often. Come to think of it, I've never really blown myself up at all. I'm still the only person who I completely trust to make the perfect bacon sandwich, with mustard and Marmite of course and toasted cheese.

I can just about grill a steak, although I can never get chips right, and I can grill a trout. I catch enough of the spotty things and I've been stuck in the middle of some God-forsaken wilderness in Scotland, Ireland or even northern Russia enough times with just my day's catch between me and starvation to have had to learn how.

In Canada and Alaska the shore lunches after a hard morning's fishing are one of the great highlights of the day. The Indian and Eskimo guides up there, way, way above the forty-ninth parallel, have methods of cooking up freshly caught lake trout that look incredibly simple. Of course a lot of it is to do with the fresh air and the magnificent scenery all around – but they appear just to chuck them into a really hot frying pan full of butter and add a few onions. The Indians make it all look too easy and, in theory, it is. But if you try it on your own, more specifically, if I try the fresh trout, bit of butter, straight into the pan routine on my own, it all ends up in a sticky black goo on the bottom.

Back in 1983, I was contracted to make a series of summer shows for TV-am and a reporter friend of mine on *TV Times* rang up to say, 'Chris, we've got to do a promotional piece about "Tarrant's Summer". Let's do your favourite barbecue.'

'I don't have one,' I said. 'I only do toasted cheese sandwiches.'

'No, no, no, that's no use at all,' she replied, never one to let a single grain of truth stand in the way of a good story. 'You're a fisherman, we'll find you your favourite way of barbecuing trout.'

'But I don't have one,' I bleated. 'I just chuck them in a frying pan and they come out all burnt and tasting like something you find on your lawn the morning after Guy Fawkes night. I only do toasted cheese sandwiches.'

'Don't be so wimpy,' she told me. 'You do a barbecued trout and you do a very good one. In fact, you do a whole exciting variety of them. Now get a silly loud shirt on – God knows you've got plenty of those – and get round here at six o'clock sharp. I'll book a photographer.'

So, sure enough, with some tenuous link to the series of summer shows that I was due to start the next Monday, there appeared a picture of me, in a loud Hawaiian shirt, looking in total control behind a sizzling, sumptuous barbecue. The article alongside was about how much I loved cooking, particularly trout and salmon, with no less than ten of my favourite recipes. Not only that, but not one of the ten was bung it in a frying pan, cover it in a pound of butter, leave it until it's black as soot and give it to the

nearest cat. There was no mention of my best technique at all!

We got away with it – or so I thought. I did a very nice series of early morning reports for TV-am from all over the UK, including an extraordinary item from a picturesque hotel in the highlands of Scotland where they had a 'trust the guest' open drinks cabinet after midnight! Anyone who ever offers a 'trust the guest' open drinks cabinet to a film crew anywhere in the world is clearly a very well-meaning human being, but sadly away among the pixies. My apologies – I digress.

We thought we'd just about got away with this piece of harmless but obligatory publicity nonsense, until I got back home and started wading through my post bag. There were requests from all over the country. Admittedly there always are some (like ''ere, Tarrant – why don't you f*** off and die?') but these were all along a whole new theme.

'Dear Chris, I was so interested in the article about your ways of cooking trout in the *TV Times*. Have you got any more?'

Or, even worse: 'Dear Chris, I was fascinated by your recipes for trout, but will they work equally well with mackerel?'

For God's sake! I don't know! I was only doing a contractually obligatory photograph. To compound my misery, I'd left TV-am by then and all these letters were being re-directed to Capital Radio. I stalled them all for weeks – then one arrived that said, 'If you don't reply to my letter and send me a recipe by return of post, I'll ring Kenny Everett'!

This was my nightmare of nightmares. Dear little Kenny, who was a seriously good cook, was also dear wicked little Kenny, who knew my skills as a chef were on a par with my abilities as a dress maker and would have had a field day. My masquerade as a cordon bleu chef would have given cuddly Ken radio material for months!

In a desperate quandary, I went to see 'Nice Norman' – a delightful but mad as a march hare figure in our press office. I told him my plight.

'No problem,' says Nice Norm. 'I love to cook. Any queries, send 'em on to me and I'll do a reply. You just sign it. That'll keep 'em all happy.'

And so it went on. Week after week, people wrote in with all their queries, Nice Norm replied and I signed it. Articles were dispatched that I knew nothing whatsoever about. Recipe after recipe was sent off with or without my blessing. I was offered a weekly cooking spot in a national newspaper, which I declined. I was even offered – and this is honestly true – my own cooking spot on a well-known daytime TV show.

The more I protested, the more exotic Nice Norm's recipes became. It was absurd but manageable until, horror of all horrors – Nice Norm left!

Still the correspondence kept coming in, usually in response to some cooking article that Norm had ghosted for me. His recipes were inspired, imaginative, mouth-watering and completely beyond me! Here's a typical example:

Truites Jurasienne

Preparation Time: 15 mins
Cooking Time: 35–45 mins
Serves 6

Clean 6 medium trout, leaving on heads and tails. Lay them side by side in a buttered oven proof dish. Peel and finely chop 2 shallots and sprinkle over the fish. Pour over half a pint of rose wine and cover the dish with buttered grease proof paper or foil. Cook in the centre of a pre-heated oven at 300F (gas mark 2) for 25 minutes.

Meanwhile, make the hollandaise sauce by boiling 3 tblspns of white wine vinegar and 1 tblspn of water with 6 black peppercorns and 1 bay leaf in a small saucepan until reduced to 1 tblspn. Leave to cool. Cream 3 egg yolks with half oz of butter and a pinch of salt. Strain the vinegar into the eggs and set the bowl over a pan of boiling water. Turn off the heat. Whisk in 5 oz of butter (quarter oz at a time) until the sauce is shiny and has the consistency of thick cream. Season with salt and pepper and add nutmeg to taste.

When the trout are cooked, lift them carefully onto a cloth and remove the skins. Strain the cooking liquid and reduce it by fast boiling until there are only 2–3 tblspns left. Let this cool slightly, then stir it into the warm hollandaise sauce. Finally, sit in 1 tblspn of double cream and garnish with bread croutons and chopped parsley.

They were incredibly detailed recipes and almost certainly delicious, but a lot more complex than a toasted sandwich.

And still the mail keeps coming in. Come back Nice Norm – wherever you are!

Just a few days ago I received yet another letter from

a terribly nice sounding lady called Mrs Pantridge from Liskeard in Cornwall.

It said, 'Thank you so much for your marvellous recipe for truites jurasienne. My husband came home with two trout the other evening and I cooked them as you instructed. They were absolutely delicious, but a little too spicy for both our palates. Do you think I may have overdone the nutmeg?'

I don't know how to break this to you, Mrs Pantridge, but I haven't got the foggiest idea!

A Quiet Bar in Ireland

Hundreds of the happiest weeks of my life have been spent in Ireland, north and south. It's a country which continues to produce some of the kindest but daftest people in the world. I mean that with genuine affection.

A couple of years back I was in southern Ireland with my constant fishing companion, Mick Fazboy the fat – so called because of his frankly hideous unhealthy plumpness – and in just seven days we managed to sample every eccentricity that this most hospitable of countries has to offer.

We were near to Shannon. For once, the fishing was really hard and we retreated to a nice little pub in the middle of absolutely nowhere. Except, of course, it wasn't really in the middle of nowhere. Standing on the original old stone floor by the peat-burning stove and looking out

of the window down across the rock-strewn fields towards the wild waters of Loch Ree, you could be forgiven for believing that you were totally isolated. We were actually only fifteen miles from the big town of Athlone where the jukeboxes in the cafes were playing the *Spice Girls*.

If you talked to the regulars in that bizarre pub, you'd think you'd stepped into another age. The locals simply could not adjust to the fact that Athlone was only about half an hour away by car. In fact, we weren't much more than an hour from Dublin, but most of the pub's inhabitants had never, ever been, nor even contemplated going.

One old farmer talked to me a lot about 'that far country', which I assumed to be England, but eventually it transpired that by 'that far country' he meant the other side of the Loch from where we were fishing, a round journey of perhaps forty miles. Neither he, nor his father, had ever made it.

The idea of coming from London that same day – even though we were only an hour and forty-five minutes by plane and rental car from Heathrow – was completely beyond them.

The landlady, a marvellous old woman of something over eighty years of age was still as fit and as tough as a prize fighter and yet as mad as a trumpet. Her pub is still lit by candles. None of that new-fangled electricity nonsense for her. And even the mere mention of a television set could lead you to being asked to leave her hostelry, possibly never to return. It was rumoured that there had once been a husband, but he was long gone and never openly mentioned. Certainly, there had once been

a someone because there was a daughter to prove it. She was a rather silent, wild-eyed and frankly terrifying looking creature called Maggie, who we all tried hard not to get served by. Although decades past her sell by date, she was clearly an absolute raver given half a chance. I swear that sometimes I could see smoke coming from underneath her frock!

One night, when we were full to bursting with the local Guinness, Fazboy The Even Fatter had tried in all innocence to give 'Ma' a goodnight peck on the cheek by way of saying thanks for a great evening, and she'd been outraged.

'Don't you be giving me your kisses, you creature of the devil. I'll have no man's kisses on my lips.' Then, in a frenzy before her cowering clientele, she hissed at Fazboy, 'You stay away from me – I'm not the kissing kind.'

Still raving, she added, 'Take her, if you must – the baby,' pointing to her trembling daughter. 'She's the one for the kissing.'

So Fazboy, anything to oblige and doing his unselfish bit for Anglo-Irish relations, gave the steaming daughter a polite peck, at which point she grabbed him in a headlock that would have done Hulk Hogan proud, and almost disappeared, tongue first, lace-up boots and all, down Mick's throat. Maggie, the 'baby' of the family, certainly was the one for the kissing, even though she was fifty-eight years old!

We stayed away, understandably, for a couple of days, out of sheer cowardice, but finally, unable to resist the

joys of such a splendid tavern any longer, we just had to pop back one more time on our last night.

Fazboy claims to be Irish, or at least he does whenever he's over there, even though he left Virginia, Co. Mayo, some time before his third birthday and sounds about as typically Irish as the 'Singing Postman', to my continuing embarrassment. This night was no exception and, as soon as he'd had a pint of Guinness and a couple of whiskeys (Irish, of course!) he started sounding off in a loud voice which he thought was typically Irish and would endear him to the locals.

It was an accent somewhere between Kenny Dalglish and Dale Winton, and was utterly incomprehensible to everybody in the little pub, including myself and I've been through the whole cringe-making business many, many times before.

'Okay, lads. Sure now, and who'll be having a wee dram with me of the hard stuff, bejeebers, och aye and Paddy Mcginty's kilt?" he enquired of the stunned silence all around him. 'Uh, come on, lads, be Jaysus, long may your lum reek, long may your sporran squeak, er . . . to be sure now, who wants what?'

I helpfully provided sub-titles. 'I think Mick wants to buy a round.'

The scales fell from the locals' glazed eyes and they realized that the fat Englishman wanted to treat them all to a drink! They needed no second bidding.

'Thank you Fazboy.'

'You're a great man Mick.'

'Large Powers here and a pint of lager for the wife.'

'Two Black Bush, a Guinness and three pints of lager.'

'Two vodkas, a gin and tonic, four pints of Guinness and a steak and kidney pudding for the donkey tied outside – you're a great man Big Faz.'

And so it went on, with Faz happily pouring out the contents of his fast dwindling wallet shouting out things like, 'It's great to be home, lads' and, 'Let's forgive and forget all about Glencoe' over the noise of the orders at the bar.

It was a great night and, even though Faz was clearly being taken to the cleaners, the atmosphere was tremendous. Or, as the Irish themselves put it, 'the crack was mighty'!

All except, that is, for the one barren corner of the bar by the peat-stove where three sour-looking creatures remained totally unmoved by Mick's generosity and continued to sit unsmiling on their own. They had big black Quaker-type hats, a full beard apiece and took it in turns to puff away at an old clay pipe. They slowly sipped their pints of Guinness through their thick froth-encrusted whiskers and sat sullenly smoking and ignoring all the other increasingly loud men around them.

Fazboy, intent on buying the entire pub a drink, didn't even notice the fact that these three were coldly ignoring him. In the end, having bought a round for almost the whole of western Ireland, he said to the amused old landlady, 'Okay, just those three in the corner, the bearded lads. C'mon boys, what'll it be? More Guinness, a whiskey if you want?'

The bearded lads drank on and puffed their pipes without even looking up.

'Ma', with great tolerance, took Fazboy on one side and said, 'Save your breath, Mick. They'll not drink with you, and they'll take no drink from any man . . . for those are the mountain women of Drumshanbo.'

Cooking Can Be Hazardous To Your Health

Ever since I met my wife, Ingrid, we've spent a lot of time in restaurants. Not particularly because she likes to be wined and dined non stop – though of course she likes to eat out in style once in a while like any other woman – but mainly it's because her cooking is so awful. That's not strictly accurate – it's not as good as awful, it's absolutely appalling. This is a woman who can burn soup to a crisp. This is a woman who can burn peas. This is a woman who can burn boiling water. Let's just say that her style of cooking is not so much cordon-bleu as cordon noir! I've suggested she bring out a book called A Hundred and One Ways of Cooking With Soot!

Statistically, most accidents happen in the home. Statistically, all of Ingrid's accidents happen in the kitchen. She once managed to set herself on fire while boiling an egg. The egg, for no reason that anyone ever really understood, exploded, splattering the walls and ceiling with the scalding remnants of what could have grown up to be a very nice chicken. Ingrid, dismissing oven gloves

as unnecessary and unladylike, pulled the sleeves of her dressing gown down over her hands to remove the red-hot two handled saucepan full of exploded egg and shell from the lighted gas hob.

'At first,' she says in a rather poetic way, 'I thought the rays of early morning sunlight were dancing upon me . . .'

Then she realized the rather more mundane reality that flames were licking up her arms and she was on fire.

Modesty hurled aside, she stripped off and, naked as a jay bird, proceeded to dance up and down on the blazing dressing gown to stamp out the fire. It was a bizarre spectacle to say the least, but at least it put a smile on the postman's face for the rest of the day.

This sort of behaviour isn't confined to her own kitchen. it's any kitchen, any time, any place, anywhere. We once took our whole tribe of kids on a canal-boat holiday to the South of France – one of our more successful family holidays. The weather was brilliant, the French countryside magnificent and the kids worryingly close to being well-behaved. Mainly we lived on salads and huge chunks of French bread and cheese, washed down with (a) gallons of lemonade for the under elevens, and (b) gallons of cheap French plonk for the over elevens.

It was all going alarmingly well until about the sixth or seventh night when Ingrid decided she was going to treat us all to a cooked chicken. Groans from all the kids, a cowardly 'That'll be really nice, darling' from me and we all went ashore, or abank, or whatever you call the bit next to a canal, to show Johnny Foreigner how cricket

is played, while Madam locked herself away downstairs in the galley with two large French chickens – long dead and well and truly plucked – on the calor gas stove.

Now, I don't know quite what happened next and quite probably none of us will ever know. One minute we were all happily playing cricket – with me being David Gower not out on 398 and all the kids plus a bewildered little French man racing to all corners of the canal-side meadow as I carved into their hostile tennis-ball bowling – and the next thing there was the most enormous explosion and the long boat's kitchen window blew out. Thorough nuisance when I was just about to notch up my fourth century, but we raced inside the boat to find Ingrid looking not unlike Eddie Murphy, with just her crazed eyes peeping out of an otherwise completely blackened face and exploded chicken all over the walls and ceiling of the galley.

She obviously has some sort of anti-chicken fetish, and if she doesn't blow them to smithereens at the egg stage, she blasts them into oblivion when they're fully grown.

By way of explanation, Ingrid said, 'I don't know what I did wrong. The gas didn't light properly so I put my head right inside the oven to make sure the gas jets at the back were re-ignited. There was a massive bang and I seemed to take the full force.'

I know, of course, it's one of those things that could happen to anybody, but for some reason it only ever seems to happen to Ingrid.

She had double vision for several days – so did I, but that was the cheap plonk – and had to wait some time for

her eyebrows to grow again. Otherwise there was no real damage – except to the boat, the chickens, the plates, the oven and our dinner. (Incidentally, we all settled for salad, bread and cheese again, and were very happy to do so for the rest of the fortnight.) After a visit to Moorfield's eye specialist hospital in London, a hairdresser who cropped the rest of her smouldered hair into a sort of Gazza-look and some busy work with an eyebrow pencil and false lashes, all visible signs of Ingrid's ordeal were quietly removed on our return. But, for the rest of the family, our scars remain. The kids say things like, 'No, no, no, Mum – let us treat you to tea tonight', but it's a recurring cry that's not heeded anything like enough.

Our house always has the smell of cordite in the air. We have sprinkler alarms all over the house, but it would be pointless putting one in the kitchen – it would be going

off all the time. the local firemen might as well move full-time into our spare room!

Lots of romantic couples have dimmer switches in the bedroom for obvious reasons, but we have them in the dining room so that, depending on just how grim the evening meal is, we can make it less and less obvious to our guests just how bad what they are about to receive really is.

Christmas day one year was an exceptional disaster. Ingrid had been busy preparing the lunch the night before – always a bad sign. Don't know why. Just always is.

Late on Christmas Eve she'd been busy peeling sprouts and as the fridge was absolutely jammed to the rafters, she left them outside the back door to cool for a while in the cold of the December night. She went to bed with total confidence that everything was in hand.

When the kids piled down the next morning, she already had the turkey in the oven and potatoes boiling away prior to roasting. Later, the kids, dog, three cats, hamster, guinea pig and Dad were all in the garden field-testing a new giant super soaker, when there were screams from the kitchen. Putting the boiled potatoes out to cool, she'd discovered the sprouts that she'd forgotten to bring back in the night before. They were transparent with frost bite and mysteriously deformed. On closer investigation, she also found strange little black objects all over them – mouse droppings!

She tried draining them in a colander with holes big enough to drain away the droppings, but the whole lot formed into an unrecognisable green mush and ended up in the bin.

At that point, Ingrid reckoned the potatoes were now cool enough to come in. Another scream, louder than the first. Bimbo, our Golden Labrador, was standing by the saucepan, licking her lips with not a potato in sight. Later on that day the dog was, of course, sick all over the house.

Christmas lunch itself was hysterical. We managed to get all our in-laws so legless before the meal that they didn't seem to notice that lunch was turkey, turkey, turkey, more turkey and gravy. It was not a good day to be vegetarian.

As an extra party piece, when Ingrid brought in the flaming Christmas pudding she set light to the table cloth and the front of her shirt as well.

Oh yes, and in the afternoon I had to retire to bed and was violently sick for forty-eight hours. The doctor said it was some sort of virus, but I was never a hundred per cent convinced.

I never used to work on Christmas Day – I fought tooth and nail not to do a live radio show on Christmas morning, but for the last five years I have done one quite happily. In fact, I volunteer. It's a good morning to be out of the house!

In fairness, I think that Ingrid's just on a run of bad luck. The fact that, to my certain knowledge, it's been running since the mid seventies is neither here nor there. And I have to concede that there was one dinner party quite recently when she did everything right. The food was disarmingly tasty and the guests were making appro-

priate lip-smacking noises. There wasn't even a hint of acrid smoke in our nostrils. It all seemed to be going much too well. Then, as our smugly beaming hostess served a delicious looking dessert – God knows how she managed it – our giant, antique dining table completely collapsed! Cream, meringue, cheese, grapes and scalding hot coffee flew everywhere. Crystal glasses shattered. Wine, port and brandy was tragically lost forever. And when one of the guests got home she found three potatoes, a tomato, a knife, spoon and a butter dish in her handbag.

The Pike That Ate a Horse and Cart

I've fished all over the world for pike. The biggest ones I've ever heard of live in Sweden or, to be more precise, off the coast of Sweden. They live in the Baltic Sea, cruise in and out of the estuary waters and are absolutely enormous. They are also, for such an aggressive fish, surprisingly difficult to catch, mainly because they have the whole area of the Baltic to hunt in and the best bait to offer them, even in an inland lake is a live herring!

I've caught them in Canada, the USA, even a few in northern Russia. I've caught big ones on the Hampshire Avon and the River Wye in Wales. But certainly the biggest I have ever seen, and the biggest I've ever hooked and sadly lost, have all been in Ireland.

Everybody in Ireland has a pike story. You will always find the greatest density of big pike stories per person in

the bars of Ireland. You'll also find the world's biggest density of bullshit!

At first, it was very exciting to hear these mind-boggling stories of Leviathans in 'the lake just up the road', and slip down to the spot well before the sun was up the next morning to find not a sniff of the great fish that the locals swore on their pints they saw with their own eyes in that particular little hidden-away bay every single morning of their lives.

But slowly, as the tales of their great pike were never borne out by actual fishing results, the penny began to drop that maybe, just maybe, we were being had. And we certainly were, although, as always with the Irish, there was absolutely no malice in it. They were just telling me things they really thought I wanted to hear . . .

There's no doubt that there are still some huge pike in Ireland, even though hundreds have been killed to 'make the trout fishing better' – a nonsense, as all it does is produce lots of much smaller trout – and hundreds more have been killed by tourists. For years the Germans in particular used to take their heads home to mount as trophies, usually chucking the rest of the fish over the nearest bush. I think, in the main, this nasty practice has been stopped now, though the damage has already been done. Yet somehow, in spite of all this, in Ireland's rich and very large waters some very huge pike still survive. They're few and far between but, according to every Irishman you meet, there's a giant pike in every farm puddle. I think, as much as anything, it's them telling you what they really think you want to hear, but its

effect on a short Irish holiday, is to waste several of your precious days on a wild goose chase.

Over years of visiting Irish bars, I've heard it all whenever I've been silly enough to ask, 'Any pike in the lake?' I've heard of 'the pike that no line can hold' in Mullingar, the 'great fella that lives on blood and guts' below the abattoir outfall on the River Blackwater and the pike that 'eats swans whole and head first' on Loch Mask. I've heard it all, chased them all and invariably found nothing there.

But one night, in a bar in Roscommon, I met a man who I really did think had at last got it all in perspective.

'Pike stories?' he said. 'Pike stories? I've heard them all and they are, with no exception, utter rubbish.

'What is it about us Irish?' he went on. 'I've heard more absurd stories, more downright nonsense talked about huge imaginary pike over the years than I've had pints of Guinness. Utter nonsense all of it. Sure now, they mean well, but I'm sad and ashamed to say they're utter liars – all of them.'

At last, I thought. A man with the whole thing in perspective and not before time. Frankly, after all my visits to Ireland, I found it very refreshing.

'I'll tell you what, though,' he added, 'and this is as true as I'm sitting next to you. There was once a pike in Lough Derg, and didn't it used to wait for us kids at school to go to our swimming class and try and bite us by the feet?

'And didn't little Jimmy Murphy lose three whole toes to that great beast down there in the summer of 1962? And wasn't I down there one day with my dad, and didn't

we both see a great pike seize a drinking horse by the nose and drag it down into the depths of the pool in a great rush of bloody water with the cart behind it and little William from the village still sitting on the back screaming for his mammy, and didn't the whole lot get dragged into the murky waters by that great fish? And weren't there just a few bubbles and the lapping of the water on the shore where the horse and the cart and poor little William had been alive and fine only minutes before . . .'

I looked at him blankly.

'Sure,' he said, 'you'll hear a lot of rubbish talked about pike in Ireland, but that one I did see with my own eyes.'

But How Do We Stop the Fat Lady Singing?

I once recorded an item for London Weekend Television, interviewing such luminaries as Michael Winner, someone out of *Eastenders*, a Shakespearean actor and a Church of England Bishop about their views on opera. It was around the time of the 1994 World Cup, when Luciano Pavarotti's rendering of *Nessun Dorma* was high in the charts all over the world, although, admittedly, it was bought mainly by football fans who went around in terrifying skinheaded gangs chanting, 'There's only one Pavarotti.'

From these interviews I discovered something that I'd long suspected but hardly ever dared to whisper out loud

– that most people in this country can't see the slightest point whatsoever of opera. I've always agreed with that viewpoint – to me it's just a lot of usually rather overweight people singing very loudly and repetitively in a foreign language. If they sang in English at least then I'd understand what it was that I was hating so much.

It's a bizarre art form where, in a nutshell, a big fat woman gets stabbed but instead of bleeding to death she starts singing. There's the old adage that 'It ain't over 'til the fat lady sings'. This is not true in opera. A fat lady usually comes on right at the beginning and starts warbling away, usually for hours. Sometimes when some misguided TV executive decides to treat us all to opera on one of the main channels, it can completely clog up a Saturday night's prime time viewing for four or five hours. The ratings are usually zilch and pubs all over the country are absolutely packed.

If you're silly enough ever to go along and through an opera, it's even less fun. Five hours and not a custard pie or gunge tank in sight. And you're not even allowed to join in. Sometimes they give you the words in your programme, but if you try and liven things up by having a bit of a sing song, the whole of your row gets thrown out.

I do remember once seeing Faust as a kid on a school outing and, having been to the pantomime the week before, I automatically started booing and shouting 'Look out – he's behind you' when the devil came on. I was dragged out of my seat by our classics master, given a

damn good thrashing and told to sit on the bus for the rest of the afternoon.

I thought last year's award of over £70 million from the National Lottery to swell the funds of the Royal Opera House was one of the most outrageous and obscene gestures I've ever heard of, and certainly not at all the sort of charitable donation that was promised when Camelot was given the Lottery franchise. When I think of all the small charities, whose whole existence would be changed and improved beyond their wildest dreams by an award of, say, even a thousand pounds, giving away the staggering sum of £70 million to anything as elitist as the opera was an absolute farce. I'm sure that if, when we all filled in our Lottery tickets, there was a little box for us to tick off which charities we'd like our money to go to, it would go to cancer research, tick, handicapped children, tick, leukaemia, tick, Aids research, tick . . . Royal Opera House? I don't think so!

The Bathing Hole

One of the most exciting and in many ways nicest countries I've ever visited is Venezuela. It is one of the last really unexplored places in the world, a strange mixture of ancient and modern, great wealth and desperate poverty. I have never seen such an obvious contrast between rich and poor – even in Africa – as we saw in Caracas. We stayed overnight in the Hilton, which is a typical luxury

American hotel that could be any Hilton anywhere in the world. The rooms are magnificent, with mini-bar and air conditioning. You can sip cocktails by the pool in the baking sunshine and dine in the sumptuous style that Americans always demand wherever they travel. Caracas itself is a buzzing, modern city with skyscrapers everywhere and Mercedes nose to tail in the rush hour.

And yet, as you come into the city from the airport, in the hills along the roadside you pass mile after mile of the most appalling living conditions that I've ever seen. Whole families are crammed into a lean-to – a tarpaulin-covered hovel that most of us would think on the small side for a garden shed. I have seen similar living conditions before, in Africa, South East Asia and parts of the Caribbean, but never on such a large scale. It goes on for ever.

There's a lot of crime in Caracas, but with such an obvious gap between the haves and the have-nots, it's no surprise.

Inflation is galloping away with their economy. When I was there in 1994 it was running at over 1,000 per cent per annum, which is incomprehensible to a European. It meant that there was no real scale of prices for anything. Enterprising Venezuelans seemed to charge almost whatever they fancied as a likely price for any item. We stayed in one three-star hotel for over £100 for a single night. The next day we checked into a five-star hotel and paid under £30 for the same deal. It was very strange, but actually rather fun. It is still the only place in the world where I've bought a beer sitting by the pool in the morning,

and gone back for another one after lunch – only to find the price had gone up!

When I double-checked with the barman, the answer was 'inflation'. Of course!

We were glad to get out of Caracas and get into the rain forest. The whole country is dominated by the Andes mountains and the Orinoco river and it is some of the wildest, most beautiful country on earth. I'm sure we deluded ourselves, but some days as you paddled along through the thickly overgrown rivers, it was easy to believe you were the first humans to come here for centuries.

Despite the fact that it's such wild country there aren't too many dangers. There aren't many big cats, mainly mountain lions that stay up on the high ground. There are no tigers or bears. Although there are a few species of snake, they always get out of your way fast if they hear you coming. There are alligators and of course the very rare anaconda.

The anaconda is a legendary creature that is feared throughout the continent – a giant python with a massive body and a huge jaw that it can dislocate at will to enable it to easily swallow a man or a mule whole. There are ancient South American tales handed down through generations of anacondas swallowing the inhabitants of entire villages. The stories are probably a little far-fetched but you certainly wouldn't want to upset one, just in case.

One of the great pleasures in the jungle is a day with an Indian guide who shows you the country and make

you see sights and hear sounds that you simply wouldn't detect on your own. It is their land and they have been there for centuries.

After a beautiful sunny morning being quietly propelled along in an old Indian canoe, about half a dozen of us stopped on the sandy shores of a deep tributary that eventually joined up with the mighty Orinoco and had some delicious barbecued chicken and local wine for lunch. The weather in February was very hot and the guide told us it was a good place to swim. We needed no second bidding and, in an interesting range of undies, dived into the deep cool waters.

Getting back, refreshed, to the shore, I poured another glass of wine and was chatting happily away to our very amiable guide, watching my wife swimming out in the middle of the water.

'This is beautiful.' I said. 'And a swim was just what we all needed.'

Then, looking down into the dark depths of the waters, I said to him, on a whim, 'I suppose it's safe?'

'Oh, yes,' he said reassuringly. 'We swim here often, and only once this year have we seen the Anaconda.'

I got Ingrid out of that river in about ten seconds flat. I'm sure the guide must have thought I was some kind of panic-merchant, but how many times do you need to see an anaconda in your regular bathing-hole before you cross it off your list of great places to swim?

Fishing Can Kill

Anybody who ever tells you that fishing is relaxing has no idea what they're talking about. Okay, you do get to fish in some beautiful remote places far away from traffic jams, phones and faxes, but it is not relaxing to spend a long day with salmon leaping all over the river and not a single one of them so much as looking at your fly, or with trout rising to within inches of your waders and totally ignoring you, or with huge carp swimming over your lovingly-prepared bait as if it wasn't even there. It's absorbing but frustrating and often ultimately infuriating. It's more fun than going to work, of course – anything's more fun than that – but relaxing it isn't.

It's also downright dangerous. I'll grant you that it's probably not quite in the same grim-reaper league as

driving a Formula One racing car or hang gliding but it's hazardous nevertheless. In August 1997 pictures of my battered and plastered body ended up in every single national newspaper when I fell, rather spectacularly, out of a tree overlooking the Hampshire Avon. I smashed my leg in, I needed several stitches to close the deep gash over my right eye, and I fractured my arm in two places. I had to put up with merciless ribbings from all my fellow DJs and listeners on Capital Radio. I even got a 'Get Well Soon, it happens to the best of us' card from Humpty Dumpty! And, sadly, that wasn't an isolated incident. Over the years, in the pursuit of big fish, I've knocked myself out, I've broken a leg, I've nearly drowned and I've electrocuted myself. All this just to catch a few fish. Was it worth it? Of course it was!

When we first moved to live by the River Mole in Surrey, even though the kids could all swim, I gave each one of them a real ear-bending about staying away from the edge, treating the river with respect, etc. It is very deep and in the summer very weedy. I wanted them to be careful. So who was the first person to fall in, and is in fact still the only one of us ever to have fallen in? Me!

I was mucking about by an old willow tree one hot afternoon, trying to clear a few weeds to make a better fishing spot, when all of a sudden the bank caved in and I went crashing into the Mole like a deranged water buffalo. I went straight under, fully clothed, and came out with great lumps of green weed all over me. Feeling distinctly silly, I went back up to the house only to find that my wife was yapping away on the telephone to one

of her friends – something she seems to do from the moment she opens her eyes in the morning, or possibly even before they open!

So, Ingrid was chatting away when this ridiculous apparition appeared in front of her, trying to attract her attention through the window. I was completely drenched, with green pond-weed all over me and was pointing to myself in a series of manic gestures. Ingrid half regarded me and carried on talking. Eventually, with a rather pained expression, she said, 'I'm sorry – I'd better go. Chris has done something.'

I certainly had.

'Well, what's up?' she said, staring at me oddly.

'Well, what do you thinks up?' I replied, rather testily. 'Observe your man.'

'You look different,' she said.

'Of course I do,' I'm forced to agree. 'Of course I look different.'

'I know,' she said, in all seriousness, 'you've had your hair cut.'

Aaaggghhhh!

I remember once spinning for pike with a friend in a one-man canoe, right on the top of the very big ancient weir at Worcester. Being schoolkids, and it being a one-man canoe, the two of us had squeezed into this precarious little thing. In a moment of madness, so that we could cast farther, we both decided to stand up. Exit me over the front and him over the back, and in a matter of seconds both of us and the now empty canoe were pouring straight over the weir and into the raging pool beneath.

FISHING CAN KILL

Anyone who's ever seen the Old Diglis Weir at Worcester will wonder how we ever got out alive. I still don't know how we managed it. We were both dragged straight under a roaring white maelstrom of water, tossed about like rag dolls and somehow spewed out again on separate banks of the River Severn about 300 yards apart. We lost the borrowed canoe and, even worse, we lost all our fishing tackle. That was our only real regret. As kids of about thirteen, the fact that we could so easily have drowned didn't bother us at all. But I think about it now and I shudder.

My experience of fishing is that it is positively perilous. I once fell head first out of a tree in Warwickshire, terrifying the fish that I had been watching underneath and knocking myself out on a log as I entered the water. Luckily, it was only inches deep and I just lay there in the muddy shallows until I came round.

I've also caught myself deep in the cheek with a fly, and had to go to a rather puzzled nearby dentist to get it removed.

As schoolboys, a friend of mine was hit by a golf ball and is lucky to be alive while fishing a lake in the middle of the golf course in Worcester. We'd got permission to fish the lake on the eighth hole until the morning golfers started at nine o'clock – only somebody decided to start at half past eight!

I've been forced off the river – and very happy to leave I was, too – by a bear in northern Canada. I've had to jump into the River Blythe to escape a completely enraged bull in Warwickshire.

I was even electrocuted while fishing a couple of summers ago in Saskatchewan. We suddenly found ourselves stuck miles from anywhere in the middle of a violent storm. The rain absolutely poured down, the sky was black as night, thunder crashed all around us and the sky was lit up every few seconds by tremendous flashes of forked lightning. Of course it was at this precise moment that a huge carp picked up my bait and tried to pull my rod in.

Cursing the fish for its lousy sense of timing, I dived out from the rocks we were trying to shelter behind and, with the rain absolutely bouncing off my bare head, grabbed my rod, only to get a great jolt up my arm. At first I thought I'd been struck by lightning, but then I realized that if that had happened, I would be toast by now. So it was clear that I was just getting a series of shocks running up my carbon fishing rod from all the electricity in the air. It was a seriously frightening feeling.

Somehow I hurried the bewildered and actually very big fish to the bank, with shocks going up both my arms all the time. I was very, very glad to be able to put the rod down and wouldn't contemplate fishing again until long after the rain had stopped and the sky had completely cleared.

But the scary events in Saskatchewan were nothing compared to my experience on the River Kennet in Berkshire. One bitter cold winter's afternoon, having drunk rather too much coffee, I turned away from the frosty riverbank to answer the call of nature. Somehow, I managed to extricate little Tommy Tinkler from beneath the many layers of long jumpers and over trousers I was

wearing. Looking up at the wintry sky, I relieved myself – straight on to an electric fence.

I am here to tell you now that there is no pain on earth like being electrocuted straight up the tinkle box! I screamed and lay there quivering, still unzipped, for what must have been several minutes. The pain went deep into the very pit of my stomach. My balls were like two blackened coconuts for a week.

About these reports of brave men having electrodes attached to their genitals in torture chambers around the world and still refusing to reveal their platoon's secrets? Forget it. I would have told the enemy anything, where my mates were hiding, where the tanks were, where we'd hidden the Bazookas, anything rather than suffer another belt from that wicked wire.

It was, of course, a source of great amusement to all my mates, but it was easily the most agonizing experience of my life. And after all that, did I catch any fish? Who the hell cares!

Crossroads

In my ATV days, as a small cog in the great wheel of the Lew Grade empire, I was never a great fan of the soap opera *Crossroads,* but because I spent many years in the same studio bar and make-up room as the cast, I was very close to a lot of the actors and actresses.

Historically, *Crossroads* has been treated rather

unfairly and became a sort of legend of TV hell. Shakespeare it certainly wasn't, but for many years the antics of the Mortimers and the Richardsons, Benny and Miss Diane attracted a huge audience. Tony Blackburn once admitted in an interview that he always used to video record *Crossroads* – which perhaps says more about Tony than it does about the series – but in its prime, it did attract a big, devoted audience to ITV, two or three nights a week. Its biggest problem, like a lot of soaps all around the world, is that the company made it on a nightmarish schedule and above all on the cheap. This meant the poor cast were either in the studio recording or learning their lines for the next day virtually all the time. In days when the TV unions were at their most terrifyingly powerful, actors were the only people working in that very lucrative industry who were virtually unprotected against the demands of the bosses for more, more, more costing less, less, less.

I do remember that several times Equity, the actors' and actresses' union, tried to give more support to their TV members in the Midlands by appointing an Equity rep to handle the cast's grievances.

Unfortunately, the rep was almost always chosen from the *Crossroads* cast. I say unfortunately because the new Equity rep would inevitably be some poor insecure soul – as most actors are – just getting used to the idea of a nice long run in a prime-time soap potentially bringing security for several years when, within a matter of weeks, they'd pick up their script on a Monday morning to find that their character is 'unexpectedly hit by a bus', or is

'happily feeding the ducks in Selly Oak Park when he's inexplicably smashed to a pulp by a runaway ex-army tank'!

Week after week the show was made on a really tight budget and, although it was recorded in advance, there was so little time or money allowed to cover over any mistakes, that it might as well have gone out live. If great big boom microphones were accidentally lowered into the picture, right on top of Meg Richardson's head, there was seldom time for a re-take and it would be kept it in on the premise that 'the audience will never spot it'. In the main, the producers were right. So, if dear old Amy Turtle couldn't remember her lines, they would be written for her in nice big letters on the back of the menu on the table, or on the side of the big clock in the motel foyer.

The fact that, on occasion, *Crossroads* looked more like one of those plays the contestants have to put together on the *Generation Game,* was neither here nor there. If, as a very convincingly angry actor stormed out of the room to conclude an emotional scene, the whole plywood set shook as the door slammed behind him, it was all seen as part of the programme's charm. Indeed, such irresistible moments may even have been part of its success.

Successful it certainly was. At its peak *Crossroads* was getting fifteen million viewers, and the stars were recognized and frequently mobbed everywhere they went. Bearing in mind that they weren't paid a fat lot in the first place, and that they were liable to be typecast forever in the second, companies' attitudes to soap stars have always been distinctly feudal.

Compared to the pay, and spin-off earnings of similar household faces in America, the wages of British soap stars were always a joke and their rigid contracts made it very hard for them to improve their financial situation. They were totally banned from writing newspaper or magazine columns and absolutely forbidden, on pain of death on the gibbet, from ever appearing in any sort of TV commercial. In the States, the stars of *Dallas* and *Dynasty* were allowed to sign fabulous contracts for endorsements. Imagine the advertisers who would have queued up and paid up for being able to claim that their soap powder or washing machine was like the one that Meg Mortimer, Elsie Tanner or Hilda Ogden used, or that the tyres on Sandy Richardson's wheelchair were Pirelli.

A regular drinking mate of mine was Paul Henry, a big unmistakable man, formerly a Shakespearean actor and a very intelligent bloke. But because he played the woolly-hatted simpleton Benny in the series, everywhere we went people treated him like an idiot. Most of them didn't even realize they were doing it! They were probably surprised he ever went out without his woolly hat on.

'A couple of beers, please.' he'd say as we walked into a pub.

'Okay, Benny.' the bar staff would say to him, without thinking.

Then painfully and embarrassingly slowly they would ask, 'Would . . . you . . . like . . . it . . . in . . . a . . . bottle . . . or . . . on . . . draught? . . . That's . . . out . . . of . . . one . . . of . . . these . . . big . . . pumps . . . like . . . this . . . one . . . here . . .'

Paul always took it very philosophically – he knew it came with the wages. But day after day it would drive most people up the wall.

I first realized how powerful these soap operas can be when I was coming out of the studio car park one morning and walked past Birmingham cathedral. It was only about eight o'clock in the morning and yet there were police everywhere all trying desperately to contain a crowd of angry, and in many cases weeping, little old ladies. I discovered that at twelve noon that day, Meg Mortimer was going to marry a particularly unlovable character called Hugh and the scene was going to be filmed that lunchtime. Forgetting the tiny detail that it was all only 'pretend', the little old ladies were beside themselves with worry.

When they spotted me a whole gang of them came racing across as their last desperate hope to prevent the tragedy.

'Oh, Chris,' wailed one hysterical lady, her eyes red with weeping, 'you've got to stop it – he's all wrong for her.'

I mumbled something like, 'It's not real, you know', which, on reflection, was about the most dangerous thing I could have said, and beat a hasty retreat to the studio doors before I got strung up there and then by my private parts.

The scene was duly recorded later that day to wails of protest from outside the church door. Sure enough, Hugh turned out to be an absolute rotter and it all ended in an ugly divorce. If only Meg had listened to the frenzied advice being screamed through the stained glass windows,

or if only the vicar had asked the little old ladies outside if they knew of any just impediment why the marriage should not take place, it would have stopped the wedding. It would also have put an end to about two years' worth of scripts!

Even more mind boggling was the selection of wedding presents that arrived at the studios. Hundreds and hundreds of them, all of which were duly passed on to charities and local hospitals. We're not just talking boxes of chocolates and bouquets of flowers. From little old ladies all over the country came silverware, rugs and carpets, standard lamps, sheets, pillows, two double beds and, I swear, a brand new three-piece suite. It's a bit of a worry, isn't it?

Of all the legendary stories about the making of *Crossroads*, there was one famous scene where Meg and Sandy were having a conversation – or at least trying to – in the reception of the Kings Oak Motel and for no reason that anyone was quite sure, Amy Turtle was hoovering very loudly just behind them.

'Have you checked that chalet number two is empty, Sandy?' Meg asked at the top of her voice.

'Yes, it's all clear now,' Sandy shouted back, trying to compete with the noise coming from Amy's vacuum.

The sound crew were having a nightmare trying to pick up the dialogue over the noise of the carpet cleaner and the director kept screaming, 'Cut! Cut!' and starting the scene again.

'Amy's killing the scene – what the hell's going on?' he asked.

After one final attempt to somehow record Meg and Sandy's dialogue over the roaring decibels coming from Amy's machine, he screamed, 'Cut! For God sake's cut, darlings.'

The director started to race out of his control room into the studio – probably to bop Amy on the nose – when the floor manager, frantically pouring over the script, suddenly screamed in excitement and joy.

'Here it is!' he said to the gibbering producer. 'Here's the problem.'

And there, at the top of the page, were the stage instructions for that scene.

'Meg and Sandy in front of reception . . . Amy hovers in the background.'

Tin Machine

I was filming one day, back in 1995, at Heathrow Airport for London Weekend Television. God knows quite what the item was, but it involved standing next to a life-size cardboard cut-out of Michael Jackson.

We'd been talking to a couple of the lads on the scanner machines earlier in the day and they'd been chuckling about the problems motor cycling World Champion Barry Sheen was having getting through security at airports.

Barry, I'm sure you remember, was probably one of the greatest motorbike riders of all time. He was also one

of the bravest, which is probably why he kept falling off a lot, usually at speeds well in excess of 100 mph. Over his years as World Champion, Barry had managed to smash just about every bone in his body. So whenever he went past the security screens, because he'd had so many metal pins put into his body, the detectors literally screamed at his approach and security guards would come rushing from absolutely everywhere.

The security guys were laughing about this and told us that in order to get round the problem in airports where he was not as well known as he was in London, Barry carried x-rays of the wrecked and rebuilt inside of his body with him at all times so that he could point out all his metal bits.

I didn't think any more about it, but several hours later, as myself and my cardboard replica of Michael Jackson were busily doing our spoof interview, we suddenly had to stop because a metal detector was making all sorts of shrill noises all over our sound track and filming had to come to an abrupt halt.

'Oh no,' said the cameraman. 'It must be Barry Sheen.'

It turned out it wasn't Barry Sheen at all, but an Arab sheikh who'd just flown in from Kuwait, leading his vast harem through a security checkpoint. The problem was that – and I found this extraordinary – as each wife passed through the metal detector, she was setting off the alarm because each one was wearing a chastity belt. The sheikh had seven wives, so seven chastity belts meant seven screaming metal detectors.

The badge is bigger than the jacket. Note the sticky out ears. I managed to flatten them in later life by sheer weight of hair!

Inset: Me at the age of three. Notice how, even at a very early age, I already looked incredibly gormless.

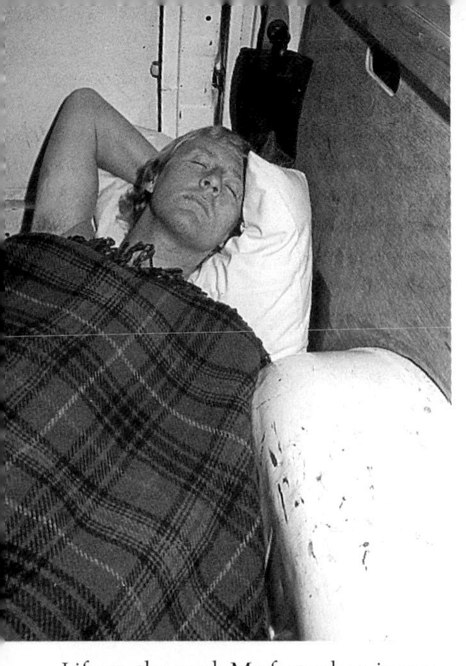

An early publicity shot of me with a particularly cheesy grin.

Life on the road. Me fast asleep in my mini van in my teaching days. Clearly exhausted after a hard night's marking.

This is me doing what I do best. The fish is big, but could it eat a horse and cart?

The producer looking thoughtful. Bob and Sally looking sensible. Lenny looking completely deranged. (Central TV)

The cage and the producer in full cry. To think people would get dressed up especially for this moment before they came into the studio! (Central TV)

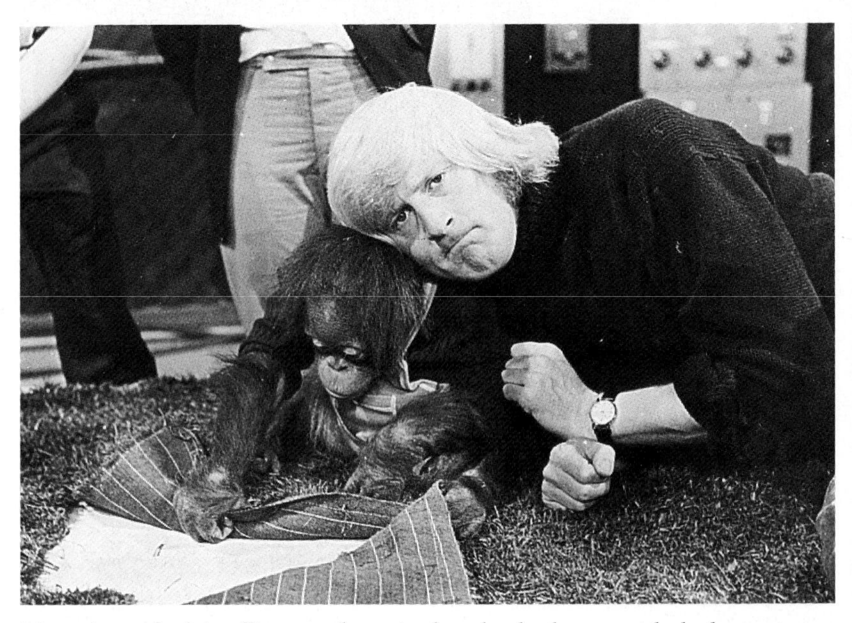

Me trying to look intelligent and pensive but clearly the one with the brains is on the left! (Central TV)

A publicity shot for me joining TV-am in 1984. A fetching little outfit, I think you'll agree, but why didn't Nick and Anne have to wear one of these too? (Universal Pictorial Press & Agency Ltd)

The new loud voice in London's ears. (Capital Radio)

With Jimmy Greaves (spot the sideboards) talking to Mohammad Ali, the greatest boxer of all time.

Note the hi-tech TV set! (LWT)

I've got the hair, but he's got the money! (Capital Radio)

Me with the lifeguards on Bondi Beach, Sydney. This is the closest I ever got to an audition for *Baywatch*. (Capital Radio)

Surrounded by lots of lovely ladies on the set of *Man-O-Man*. It's a tough job but someone's got to do it! (Reg Grundy Productions)

Winner of both New York Radio Awards for 1996. At this proud moment I was apparently 'the funkiest man on the planet'. (Capital Radio)

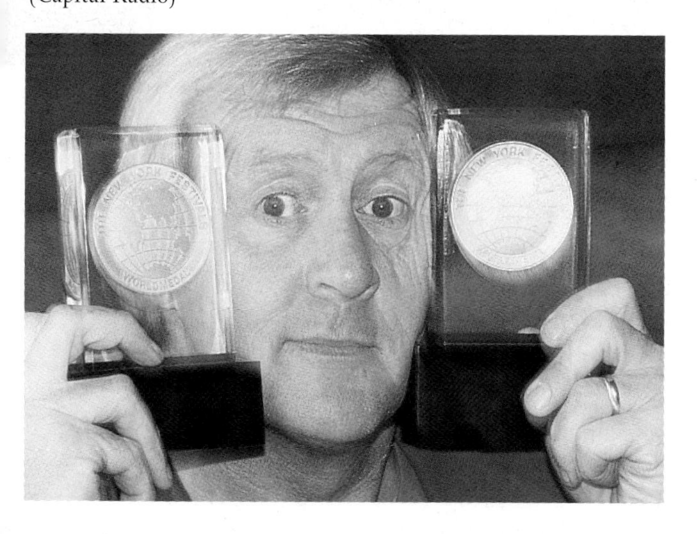

Lost for words for probably the only time in my life when Mike produced the big red book. (Kentish Times Newspapers)

Jumping in the air outside Capital Radio, celebrating the signing of my new contract to the year 2000! Clearly looking forward enormously to the sheer joy of another three years of 5 a.m. alarm calls. (Capital Radio)

Living happily well out of the Middle East, I found it incredible that in 1995 men still had harems, let alone be allowed to clamp those medieval iron 'defenders of purity' on all their women.

The Middle East is really not very far away these days, as the jumbo jet or missile flies, but it's still very much another world. Just think, there are still plenty of us in this country who grumble about being forced to wear seat belts!

Sign, Sign, Sign

I don't know how many autographs I must have signed in the twenty odd years since I first started being on the telly but it must be thousands and thousands. It's really no big deal. I think that if you gave a stuffed bear its own TV show, every day for a couple of weeks, it would start to get fan mail and requests for signed photos by about the first Wednesday!

Over the years, one way or another I've signed all sorts of things: nice neat autograph books, postcards, bits of school exercise books, family allowance books, cheque books, T-shirts, brassieres, bus tickets, bog rolls, arms, back, stomachs and far, far worse. More of which later.

I'm sure the great majority of autographs are lost or thrown away almost at once, but I cannot for the life of me understand so-called celebrities who won't sign them. It is your audience who pay your wages, and as long as

they ask in a reasonably pleasant, normal way, it's the very least you can do. There haven't been many occasions when I've refused but, I do remember the first time I didn't sign one.

I was doing a live TV show at the Royal Showground, near Kenilworth, and once we'd finished I was happily signing away for a very sweet bunch of ten and eleven-year-olds and their very pretty teacher, when suddenly a great shaven headed oaf of about seventeen or eighteen pushed straight through all the kids, stuck a bit of paper under my nose and said in a loud leering voice, 'Sign that, tosser!'

Needless to say, I didn't feel I was absolutely duty-bound to sign it. I'm six foot two, so I stuck him fairly firmly back where he came from, at the very last place in the queue and made him lose a lot of face in front of the younger kids. He was an exception. In the main, people are really nice.

Signing autographs is also quite a good way of getting feedback, of learning what they like and what they don't like about whatever show you're currently doing. I remember the first day we ever used Spit the Dog on Tiswas. I went to an open air carnival the next afternoon and signed hundreds of bits of paper. all the mums were moaning at me because their kids had been making nasty spitting noises at their brothers and sisters, while cleaning their teeth that morning. Of course I couldn't appear to approve, so I apologized to them all profusely and tut-tutted dutifully, but secretly I knew we had a big hit on our hands, or, to be more precise, a big spit!

I'll never forget that particular afternoon because the carnival organizers had me sat at a nice table with a couple of beers in the sunshine as a long queue of kids and their mums patiently waited for 'the man to sign your programme'. I was chatting to most of them as they came up about this and that – mainly Spit the Dog – when one dear little boy of about five came up with his mother.

'Hello, little man,' I said. 'What's your name?'

'Simon,' he whispered, and tried to hide behind his mum.

'Okay,' I said, and signed, 'To Simon, best wishes . . .', etc., on his bit of paper.

'And who's this?' I said to the shy little boy. 'Is this your mummy?'

'Yes,' he said.

'And is she nice?' I asked.

'Yes,' he said, and then added in a much louder voice, to the delight of the eavesdropping crowd, 'but my daddy says she makes smells in bed.'

The poor woman went absolutely scarlet.

Then of course there are always the mums and dads who come up pretending the autograph's not for them anyway.

'It's not for me, it's for the kids.'

'It's not for me, it's for my friend at work.'

My favourite is still a bloke who with a totally earnest face said to me outside Capital Radio a couple of years ago, 'It's not for me, honest. I think you're crap.'

One extraordinary memory is of a little seven-year-old girl who came up to me once for an autograph in a similar queue when I was crowning the May Queen in Uttoxeter. She trotted up with her father, we were chatting away happily and I was just about to sign her poster when her big grinning father said, 'Go on, Tarrant, sign her one of your cheques, for a laugh.'

So I said all right. I'd done it before, several times. It's actually quite a nice keepsake for the little girl and probably likely to last longer than the average bus ticket. Quite recently, I met a woman who was about twenty-eight, and who still had a cheque framed from when I'd signed it for her when she was a little girl in the seventies.

I signed the cheque: 'Pay Tracey one million pounds . . . Chris Tarrant', and she went happily away.

On the Tuesday, I got a call from the manager of the West Bromwich branch of Barclays Bank.

'Er, Mr Tarrant?'

'Yes,' I said.

'Well, it's a bit embarrassing, but there's a man in here who's just presented us with a cheque for a million pounds against your current account.'

Needless to say the cheque bounced and I never was silly enough to sign one like that again. But what a let down.

I've signed autographs in total darkness in discos – God knows what they say when they're read in daylight the next morning. I've signed one in thick fog up the top of Mount Snowdon, another while trying to make my way very precariously down a ladder, and I've signed them lots of times in gents' lavatories even though it's fairly obvious that I'm rather pre-occupied at that precise

moment and need both hands. Well, okay, one hand anyway!

I remember once that I'd just caught a lunchtime flight out of Heathrow to Madrid with only minutes to spare. I'd got into my seat and the plane had taken off as soon as I'd got my safety belt on. It had been a hectic few days and I was absolutely shattered. I had a quick scotch, asked the very nice hostess not to bother about giving me anything to eat, and crashed out in a really deep sleep.

We'd probably only been flying for about half an hour or so and I was absolutely out for the count, when somewhere deep in my consciousness I felt a sharp poking in my chest. Then I felt it again – but firmer and more urgently. When I eventually managed to open one eye there was a completely strange woman looming over me, sticking a bit of paper under my nose saying, 'Sign this for my two kids, please – Rachel and Donna.'

Why Rachel and Donna's mother couldn't wait until I'd woken up properly I'm not quite sure. After all, we were all going to Madrid and I was hardly likely to jump out and free fall parachute over the Massif Central, was I?

I signed it anyway because, as I said earlier, it comes with the territory.

But it was as nothing compared to what happened in Great Yarmouth.

We were doing a week of shows in East Anglia one summer. Arriving early on the Sunday evening while the director and camera crew were going through a very tedious meeting about the technical requirements for the next

day's programme, Mike Purcell, the unit manager and I decided we'd go and have a couple of quiet beers and maybe meet a few good old Norfolk locals.

But when we opened the door to a nice looking old tavern we found that we had walked into the pub from hell. There was not a sign of good Norfolk locals. Presumably they'd all drunk up quickly and done a runner hours ago because the pub seemed to hold the entire population of Glasgow.

We learned too late that, up in Scotland, it was industrial holiday fortnight, and it seemed that the whole lot of them had come charabanc upon charabanc to this tiny bar in Great Yarmouth. And of course they were absolutely legless. I'm a big bloke and so is Mike but everywhere we looked there were huge, hairy, tattooed, drink-crazed Scotsmen towering down on us and calling my name. They were drunk and they were big. But some of the women with them were even drunker and bigger. It was terrifying.

The crowd more or less carried the two of us to the bar and forced pints of McEwans down us. We shook their hands, we politely kissed their women, trying not to offend anyone or quite look anyone directly in the eye in case it all went horribly wrong. I signed beer mats, I signed raffle tickets, big hairy arms, anything just to stay in one piece. It was one of those situations that seemed like a great laugh – but any second could suddenly have switched to flash point and ended up with a bottle in someone's forehead – probably mine.

When a lady came up, lifted up her top and produced

her naked breast for me to sign I thought, this is it, I'm going to die! At that moment her great hairy husband came out of nowhere and instead of head butting me and nailing my three-piece suite to the dart board, he positively insisted that I sign his very nice wife's bare breast (her 'tut' as he so quaintly called it) which I obligingly did to the wild whooping applause of the dangerously drunken crowd.

'That's it,' I thought. 'Let's drink up and do a runner.'

But the baying Scottish throng had one more little demand before they decided to let me live another day.

A particularly savage-looking Jock with a great uncombed mane of red hair loomed towards me, slopping Tennent's lager everywhere.

'Okay,' he said. 'You signed that – now sign this!'

It's not an episode I'm particularly proud of, but there are times in this life when you just have to do whatever needs to be done to stay alive. Which is why, in front of the by now completely hysterical crowd chanting 'Sign! sign! sign!' at the tops of their voices like some nightmarish scene from *Lord of the Flies,* and without touching anything except my biro (I wish I'd had a fountain pen) and with both eyes firmly shut, I signed a Scotsman's plonker!

Rubber Trouser Job

Capital Radio Christmas parties have always been legends of misbehaviour. A private room full of disc jockeys, producers and the production staff all winding down for Yuletide with a free bar open all night inevitably leads to all sorts of naughtiness and thank the Lord for that! It's probably best to draw a discreet veil over the Michael Aspel, Kenny Everett early years of Capital, except to say that it is a well-authenticated fact that one well known disc jockey (neither Mike nor Kenny, by the way, before you start guessing) was caught with his willy in the office bulk eraser.

In my own years, the Christmas parties have been equally riotous, although as far as I know we managed to steer clear of sexually molesting any of the office equipment. There was the year that Irish Betty from the canteen drank enough Guinness to have kept the whole of the west of Ireland drunk for twelve months, then managed single-handedly to knock down the entire cloakroom and pass out with a great crash in the middle of the dance floor. Somebody plucked up the courage to give her the kiss of life and she was rushed off on a stretcher into an ambulance.

There was a wonderful moment when our personnel lady, watching the departing form of the unconscious Betty, said, 'But why does everyone jump to the conclusion that it must have been alcohol? It could just as easily be a stomach virus!'

Yes, of course, it could – and the moon is made of camembert!

There was the year I decided to demonstrate my lambada skills and, crazed with the brown ale, decided to make the dance even more impressive by picking up a huge twenty-stone producer, Paul Pink, and carry him in my open arms as I tripped the light fantastic. 'Tripped' being the operative word. After about three steps I went down like a sack of spuds, with the huge bulk of Pinky right on top of me, neatly landing with my elbow straight on top of a beer bottle. I needed several stitches and had to press all the jingles and put on the records the next morning with only one working arm.

Of course the thing about having a Christmas party at a radio station is that all the time the party is going on, there's some poor DJ in the studio next door live on air still desperately trying to hold himself and a radio show together. Like most stations, Capital pumps it out live twenty-four hours a day, 365 days a year. So as the party gets more and more out of control there's somebody thinking, 'Oh, God – I'm on air in ten minutes. Oh, well, I'll just have the one more beer.'

A couple of Christmases ago I decided not even to try and get home for a couple of hours' kip before the breakfast show, and took a room in the hotel right opposite the studios. Having had a serious skinful, I fell into my room around three in the morning, only to find several of the girls and a couple of the DJs had also decided to use my room as a handy place to put their heads down for a few hours. I was due on air at 6.30 a.m. and Richard Allinson,

who was as drunk as a skunk, was due on at 4.30 a.m . . . in about an hour and a half's time.

I somehow set the clock for 6.15 and dived into bed, fully clothed. I think I even had my shoes on!

The alarm screamed into my ear after what seemed like only five minutes, but there was no mistake – the clock said 6.15 a.m. I felt like death, my tongue tasted like the bottom of a rhino's cage and somebody appeared to be hitting me over the head with a shovel. The room was full of people, several of whom I was sure I'd never seen before in my life, all sprawled comatose in various corners of the room. Bewilderingly, I was stripped to the waist, even my shoes had disappeared, and horrifyingly, my jeans were completely soaking wet.

'Oh, my God,' I thought. 'This is the worst day of my life. Having drunk gallons of beer last night my bladder has thrown in the towel some time in the small hours of the morning. My decrepit body has finally caved in. I am incontinent. From now on, I am a rubber trouser job!'

I had no change of clothes, so I dried my trousers as best I could with a towel, some how picked out a T-shirt and sneakers from the motley selection of garments strewn across the floor and, soaked and ashamed, raced across to the studio. By the time I got there we were into the commercial break. Allinson had been and gone. God knows what his show had been like: I suspect a lot of music with just the occasional slurred time check. I fired a jingle, cued the news and I was on.

The next three and a half hours felt like an eternity. My diction was surprisingly clear – well, about normal

anyway – despite the coating of fur on my tongue. My head stopped pounding after about an hour, several coffees and a bit of the *Eagles'* 'Tequila Sunrise'. But all the time I was sitting there, still soaked and filled with shame, knowing that after years of appalling abuse, my body had finally given up on me.

I kept hearing a voice saying, 'You are now officially incontinent. You are a rubber trouser job.'

People kept popping in and out of the studio, handing me the usual bits of paper. None of them said anything but I was sure that they knew. I was sure I could see them twitching their nostrils as they passed me in the heated studio.

And still the voice came, 'You are a rubber trouser job.'

At this point Richard Allinson came in looking like death. He was unshaven, distinctly green around the gills and his bloodshot eyes were peeping out of the sockets like two pregnant prawns.

'God, you look dreadful,' I said, forgetting my own disgraceful plight for a second. 'I've never seen anyone look so dreadful.'

'I feel dreadful,' he said. 'I've never drunk so much in my life.'

Then, rather sheepishly, he added, 'Look, I'm really sorry about the bucket of water.'

'What bucket of water?' I said.

'Well, you know. *The* bucket of water. About four o'clock we threw a bucket of water over you. I don't really know why we did it now, but the amazing thing was that you never even stirred. We took your T-shirt off, but

thought it best to leave your trousers on. You were absolutely drenched. I'm really sorry – it seemed like a good idea at the time.'

It was possibly the best news I've ever heard in my life. I hugged the bewildered Allinson, I pumped him by the hand, I may even have kissed him! I couldn't begin to explain to him how happy his mumbled apology had made me.

The rest of my radio show was a breeze. The listeners must suddenly have found me inexplicably chirpy. I put on *D-Ream*'s 'Things Can Only Get Better', wished everybody a nice Christmas Eve and left the studio with my head, and my trousers, held high.

'So Sorry . . . Strictly No Alcohol'

One summer, when the full squad of The Bucketeers were tied up all over the UK – Sally was in Portugal, Lenny was in Blackpool, Bob and Spit were in Bridlington of all places – John Gorman and I were booked for a series of two-man shows. I say 'two-man', but we also brought along a pianist mate of ours, Mike Mann. As he was the only one of us who wasn't totally tone deaf in what was a two and a half hour mainly musical show, he was something of a bonus. In fact he was totally indispensable – not that we reflected that in his minuscule wage. Certainly not.

In a frenetic fortnight we did an extraordinary mixture

of venues. Universities, of course, including one Saturday evening in Glasgow – not the most discerning of audiences but, God, did we have a great night – small theatres, a couple of dauntingly large theatres including the Liverpool Empire and several army camps. These were an education. The first one we did was on a filthy wet Friday night, somewhere on Salisbury Plain.

The first thing you quite quickly realize when trying to entertain Her Majesty's forces is that they are the most rat-arsed audiences you will ever meet on earth! Their idea of a great night out is to get absolutely paralytic and then beat lumps out of anybody who's handy. If the nearest people handy happen to be a couple of blokes off the telly then that's absolute magic. Having narrowly escaped with our lives getting away from a barracks, somewhere on the plain, John and I decided to reshape our show artistically before the next booking – Friday night in Aldershot.

In the interests of our art, and more importantly in the interests of leaving Aldershot with our bits and pieces still attached to our bodies, we cut all the sketches, all the jokes – well both of them anyway – all the songs bar one and put in loads of four lettered words. Basically, we did a two-hour extended version of the 'Bucket of Water Song', inviting one after another of Her Majesty's finest and bravest up on stage to pour water all over their uniforms and dive into a huge bath of custard while screaming obscenities at their wives, girlfriends and all the officers. Culturally, perhaps it was a little limited, but as a means of getting out in one piece, it was a masterpiece. They all

had one of the best nights of their lives and we got away without so much as a bayonet up the rectum. As we wished them goodnight the baying mob gave us a standing ovation.

In spite of an offer from a very nice lieutenant to stay and have a few drinks with the lads, John and I decided it was probably unwise to linger and made our excuses. We dived off for the nearest pub, club or anywhere that would still serve us. It was close to twelve and all we could find on a Friday night in swinging downtown Aldershot was a Chinese restaurant. However, we weren't fussy, so we parked up and dived in. It was absolutely packed, all the tables groaning with mountains of sweet and sour everything, noodles and big jugs of wine and beer. This was exactly what we needed, so just after midnight a very nice waiter found us a table for two.

We ordered a great pile of Chinese goodies, but more than anything we wanted a drink. In fact, we wanted lots and lots of drink – gallons of it. It had been a hard, if eventually triumphant night and we were seriously thirsty.

'Can we order a drink?' we asked the waiter.

'Yes, of course, Sir, but 'raid no alcohol.'

It took a second or two for the penny to drop.

'No alcohol How d'you mean no alcohol?'

'So sorry, Sir – not allowed to serve any alcohol. Plenty drink but absolutely no alcohol. So sorry!'

'Hang on,' said John. 'Can't serve alcohol. This place is awash with alcohol. Everybody's got alcohol. There's gallons of alcohol on every table.'

'Yes, Sir, plenty of alcohol, of course, but not allowed

after midnight. No licence. No alcohol after twelve o'clock. So sorry, Sir.'

This was desperate. But the more we insisted, the more he kept apologising. Clearly it was more than his job was worth to serve us with even a teaspoonful of the deadly alcohol after the witching hour. We were still going to need something, anything, to wash down the salty mountain of Chinese food we'd ordered.

'All right, then,' said John, with bitter resignation. 'If we can't have anything alcoholic, what can we have?'

'Yes, Sir, straight away, Sir, and so sorry about no alcohol. We got plenty, Sir – orange juice, Coca-Cola, diet coke, seven-up, lemonade, pineapple juice, lager, black currant juice, tomato juice . . .'

'Hang on, hang on,' I said. 'Did you say lager?'

'Yes, Sir, we got lager, black currant, lemonade. So sorry about no alcohol.'

'Yes, never mind black currant and lemonade. So if we wanted, say, a couple of pints each of this, er, lager stuff, that's not a problem then?'

'Absolutely not, Sir – lager no problem. So sorry about no alcohol.'

'Not a problem,' John said. 'We'll have seven pints each of this lager, please.'

'No problem, Sir, straightaway. Fourteen pints of lager. I go get tray. So sorry about other problem.'

So we sat there, gorging on Chinese food and drinking pint after pint of lager. In the end, after we'd drank our first order of seven pints apiece of perfectly ordinary, straightforward, very alcoholic lager, we drank some

more, and about four in the morning we drank some more after that.

We left the restaurant absolutely steaming, with the waiter thanking us profusely for a very handsome tip, still apologizing.

'Thank you, Sir. Hope you had a good night – and so sorry about no alcohol.'

'It's not a problem,' we somehow slurred in reply. 'And a good night to you, too.'

Back in our hotel we were both asleep or perhaps unconscious before our heads hit our pillows. I still have no idea what on earth our confused Chinaman was thinking of. But the way it turned out, I don't think it much matters!

Big Jack

As a teenager I used to fish a lot with a devious old poacher from the Cotswolds called Big Jack. He was a big bearded bloke with hands like shovels and a nose that, over the years, had gradually been splatted farther and farther across his face. He ate, drank and made love to anything and everything he could lay his hands on. He cooked rabbit, jugged hare, partridge, pheasant, wild goose, venison – no questions asked – crayfish, even rooks that he gathered dead off the road first thing in the morning and turned them into an absolutely magnificent pie the same evening. You had to close your eyes and think of England,

of course, but it tasted superb. He was the first person to serve me with baked hedgehog, again gathered off the Fosse Way before sunrise. The flesh was magnificent, although occasionally there was an unmistakable taste of Michelin rubber.

He also cooked lots of trout. With the Windrush, the Evenlode and the Colne on his doorstep, there were rivers full of trout everywhere. Unfortunately, most of them were extremely privately owned and very expensive to fish, if permission could be obtained at all.

Jack didn't have any money, but he managed to catch lots of trout anyway, one way or another, and, full of charm as the old rogue could be, local landowners occasionally gave him a day's fishing on their sacrosanct waters.

So I wasn't particularly surprised when one evening in the pub he told me he'd got permission to fish the local Lord of the Manor's very private stretch of the Windrush, which we always knew was full of big trout, but had never dreamed of fishing.

'Funny thing is,' said Jack, 'he'll only let us fish there after dark. It's all above board, but he doesn't want to upset any of the other locals.'

'Fair enough,' I said, gullible little soul that I must have been. 'When can we go?'

'Well, actually, he's invited us tonight!'

Two or three ciders later, as the landlord was calling last orders, off we went. It was a black night, but Jack seemed to know the way. We went up a track, parked, climbed a gate, walked around some old buildings in the dark and came down to a beautifully manicured lawn.

'This is it,' said Jack. 'He says we can fish here.'

To say the fishing was good would be an understatement. There were trout everywhere, ridiculously easy to catch, mainly on big chunks of bread and we absolutely caned them. They were huge, as well. I think the smallest we caught was over 4lb, and the bigger ones were more than double that. We went home exhausted and Jack stocked his freezer up for a month.

It was only the next day, walking through the village in broad daylight, that I realized that we'd been fishing in the private garden right in front of His Lordship's house. A discreet enquiry in the village Post Office revealed that, as it was a bank holiday, he was away in Scotland for the long weekend – coming back that night.

Apparently he went away to his estate in Perthshire every year at the same time, but didn't stay long because he liked to get home and hand feed the tame trout off the end of his lawn!

Even worse was the night that the enormously overweight Jack had been warned off beef and pork by his doctor, so he decided to go on a mutton only diet for a couple of weeks. One minute we were quietly driving home from the pub in his beat up old van, the next we'd swung in through an ancient wooden gate, head lamps full on, right across the field, inquisitive sheep coming into the beam from all around us. The first one was poleaxed squarely across the nut with a starting handle and was in the van, away home, de-fleeced and carved into thirty or forty tasty frozen dinners before you could say Hannibal Lector! I am thoroughly ashamed of the whole business

– even though I was a bemused innocent bystander. But Jack and his family didn't give it a second thought – it was simply how they lived.

The silliest night I ever spent with him was just outside Salisbury in the middle of February. The weather was bitter. We'd driven down there in my old MGB sports car, crammed to the roof with fishing tackle, food and sleeping bags, fished all day, had a few whiskies and eventually climbed into the low slung seats to get a few hours' kip before fishing again the next morning. Although it was bitterly cold, we had plenty of blankets and I was nice and cosy, falling asleep almost at once. Jack, who had a bad back, probably from years of carrying somebody else's lambs and deer over his shoulders, couldn't get comfy at all and kept waking me up with his complaining.

In the end, aching all over and totally fed up, he decided to sleep outside the car on the ground where at least he could stretch out properly.

I thought no more about it and snoozed happily on.

It was only when I opened my bleary eyes in the morning to find the passenger seat empty and the windscreen completely white with frost that I realized the insanity of what Big Jack had done.

I got out of the car and found myself staring at an apparition.

Jack was still alive but not very happy – not very happy at all. His sleeping bag was completely covered with ice, his hair and eyebrows were stiff and matted with frost and his beard was actually frozen to the ground.

'I can't move,' he mumbled through chattering teeth. 'You young bugger, get me up!'

Somehow I first had to defrost his beard. My first suggestion was, I admit, a little extreme, and even in his sorry predicament Jack was outraged and dismissed it out of hand, threatening to kill me if I came anywhere near him. So we settled for plan B which meant me diving off to the local cafe and coming back with a thermos of hot tea, which I very carefully poured around the unhappy rooted beard. It worked, of course, and he slowly got to his feet, a battered man.

I still preferred my first suggestion!

Crime Fighter Au Naturel

When Capital Radio did their much-publicized move to Leicester Square after twenty-odd years of being a known landmark along the Euston Road, it was a bit of a wrench in many ways. But because it was done quietly across the Christmas and New Year holiday period, it was all fairly painless. There is something rather exciting about being right slap bang in the middle of London.

However, parking immediately presented itself as a problem and people kept on at me about the security aspect of parking away from the building. I wasn't really aware of it, until the morning I was mugged. I say mugged, but mini-mugged would be more accurate.

Having parked my car up along the Charing Cross Road

and started to walk the few minutes to the studio, I was less than impressed when some bloke popped out of a doorway saying, 'I want your wallet, man.'

The best thing about radio is that you can bluff, and however I may sound at 6.30 a.m., at 6.29 I'm just as comatose as everybody else. At that time of the night, on a cold, black February morning, it's difficult to relate to anything and since I hadn't spoken to a single person that morning the fact that I was being mugged didn't really sink in.

My mugger seemed to understand my early morning dullness, so he repeated his request, 'I said I want your wallet, man.'

At this point I suddenly realized what an outrageous request this was and I said to him, somewhat forcibly and surprisingly articulately for that ungodly hour, more or less exactly these words.

'It's early, it's dark and it's bloody cold. I don't like my alarm clock, I don't like getting out of bed and I'd much rather be still at home lying next to my wife. The only possible reason for me to be out of bed at this time of night is to earn some money. So why on earth would I give it to you before I've even got there?'

He seemed impressed but non-plussed by my logic, so I added, 'Now sod off before I give you a smack' and he ran away!

At the time the whole episode was like a bad dream before you've properly woken up. It was only after he'd gone running off and I had walked a few more steps down the road that I realized, 'I think I've just been mugged, or half mugged, or attempted mugged, or whatever!'

I admit that, on reflection, he does appear to have been the world's wimpiest crook, but he might have had a knife, or I could have been one of the girls in our office. The point is that it's usually only after the event that you start thinking about what might have happened. At the time you just act on instinct. It's only afterwards that you worry, like when we were burgled in Lambeth.

I used to share a house with several girls in Albert Square, living in my own room downstairs. There was strictly, and sadly, no hanky panky, just a lot of tights in the sink every morning when I was trying to shave. So, when Linda, who actually owned the house, came back at two o'clock in the morning and crept into my room I didn't assume that she was after some funny business (not least because my girlfriend was with me) but that she had chosen that Godforsaken time to wake me up and give me some tedious domestic note – something dull about taking out dustbins or a man coming to read a meter.

Suddenly, the floorboards creaked and even though it was absolutely pitch black, I made out a figure standing right next to my bed and realized that it wasn't Linda at all. It was a bloke. I couldn't see him clearly, but it was pretty obvious that he was uninvited and, screaming loud obscenities like 'Who the . . . ?' and 'What the . . . ?' I jumped out of bed, completely naked, and chased the terrified bloke off along the hallway, out of the front door and out into the street. The silly thing is that I never even saw him. It really was pitch black. The street lamps had gone out and all I could hear were his panicking footsteps racing off round the corner.

It was only after I'd run a couple of hundred yards that I suddenly realized the full enormity of my situation. Here's me – two o'clock in the morning in the middle of Lambeth with not a stitch on, chasing a fully clothed and possibly fully armed burglar. God knows what I'd have been able to do if I'd caught him. I wasn't really dressed for a citizen's arrest!

Needless to say, we never caught him, even though there was a perfect set of fingerprints on the smashed front room window.

To add insult to injury, when I tried to sneak naked as a jay bird back into the house, all the girls had woken up and gave me a cringe-makingly embarrassing welcome back. All except for my own then girlfriend who was still fast asleep in our bed and hadn't heard a thing!

Laugh . . . I Thought I'd Never Start

I've never liked clowns. I'm sorry, and I know that it's just a personal thing, but even as a kid I never found them funny. They were just the boring bit that came running on while we were waiting for the lions or the seals. They were the only thing in the world that actually made you look forward to the Mongolian jugglers. Why should anyone with ludicrous make-up, bizarre hair and ridiculously loud clothes assume they're going to make people laugh? If they did, we'd all go to the big top every Christmas to see Barbara Cartland top the bill.

They're always from somewhere like the Ukraine. When did you ever meet a funny Ukrainian? And they always drive on in a car whose doors fall off and whose engine blows up and squirts water everywhere. It's not even a prop – all Ukrainian cars are like that.

Then there's always the very funny bucket-of-ice-cold-water-down-the-trousers routine. Of course the great thing about ice cold water down the trousers is that it makes men more fertile, which is why there seem to be more and more clowns at the circus every time you go. If only they would try the boiling hot water down the trousers routine instead of the ice cold version, you could wipe out the whole lot of them in one generation.

And then, just when you think it can't possibly get any worse, on comes the one in the pointed hat with bobbles

on who plays the cheap, dented, out of tune saxophone. Oh, how we laugh. And while he plays the dreadful thing, a flower grows out of his hat. Oh, ho, ho, there goes the other rib!

As the finale, there's always the classic wallpapering routine, which consists of a white faced man jabbering away in Ukrainian, falling off his ladder and running round the circus ring with one foot stuck in a bucket of wallpaper paste, looking for someone to attack with a custard pie. I know this to my cost. Last time I went to a circus, I took my little four-year-old boy, Toby. The clown spotted me in the audience and halfway through the wallpapering act, came racing over – with one foot still jammed into his bucket, of course – and hit me squarely in the face with a custard pie. Toby burst into tears, became quite inconsolable and, with me still blinking half-blindly through the custard, we had to take him home. He didn't know my history and that, frankly, over the years, his dad had thoroughly deserved it!

The promising thing is that although he was only four years old Toby had already developed a healthy aversion to clowns.

Old Peggy

I used to know this lovely gypsy lady down in Devon. A real old rogue she was, but incredibly wise, and I used to sit in her kitchen drinking home-made soup while she

chatted on to me for hours about everything under the sun.

She made a living out of selling things to people on their doorsteps: brushes, brooches, lucky charms, the lot. The old rubbish she managed to talk people into buying used to amaze me. She reckoned that, in the main, people tended to buy something just to get rid of her, and I'm sure she was absolutely right. She used to be loudly abusive to people who didn't cough up, and I'm sure that, rather than have the whole neighbourhood peeping round the curtains as this loud-mouthed Romany slagged you off as a meanie, most people would give in, if only to get her off the doorstep.

She told me very proudly that she was travelling through Scotland once and in the course of a week she sold eleven cases of lucky heather . . . !

She certainly knew a lot about people. She'd been married for something like forty-five years, and yet she was always counselling me on my confused, and mainly disastrous, love life. At that age, I used to wake up in the morning, fall madly in love by lunch-time and be fed up with the whole thing by about seven o'clock in the evening.

I'd lived with two or three girls in London, and been absolutely potty about dozens of others, but it always seemed to go wrong. They'd take exception to some little habit of mine, like bringing other women back home or keeping fishing bait under the bed, and it would all break up in bitterness and confusion.

What always struck and saddened me was how little it

all actually mattered in the end. A couple of times when my romances had broken down, for whatever reason, I'd been absolutely shattered, gone on monumental binges that lasted for days, then dripped about like a wet lettuce for weeks. I'd been sure my whole world had come apart at the seams and that there was no possible point in going on. I'd never ever look at another woman. I'd become a monk. I'd join the Foreign Legion. I'd get an allotment . . . Then one day I'd walk into the local chippy and there behind the counter would be some raven-haired beauty with a huge chest and a smell of vinegar and the whole silly business would start all over again.

One night in Peggy's kitchen, I was banging on about the impermanence of everything. She, of course, understood the whole problem.

'You're only here once and, in the end, none of it matters a damn. It all comes out in the wash . . .'

Then she told me a very simple story that somehow summed it all up in a nutshell.

Long before she'd met her husband, Peggy had fallen madly in love with a much older man, who was married with three kids. She had gone through absolute hell over this bloke for four years, sure that one day he'd leave his wife and marry her. But, of course he didn't. In the end, one night he'd told her it was all over. She was absolutely distraught, even suicidal. Sobbing hysterically, she'd gone up to one of the cliffs high above Torbay and just stood there in the wind closing her eyes, clenching her fists and willing herself to take the one step forward that would plunge her to her death.

Several times she'd looked down at the jagged rocks and the raging sea, hundreds of feet below and nearly summoned up the courage to just let herself go. But each time she couldn't quite will herself out into space . . . In the end, she'd somehow dragged herself away from the cliff's edge and gone home sadly to begin an empty life.

'And d'you know,' she said, 'I was thinking about it the other day, and I can't even remember his bloody name . . .'!

Nappy Days Are Here Again!

Why do all new born babies look like Winston Churchill?

It's like asking, why do all bank robbers with stockings pulled down over their faces look like Clive James?

If you're ever asked to judge a baby contest plead insanity, feign illness, tell 'em you're distantly related to King Herod. Make up any excuse you can – but whatever you do, don't do it!

Years ago, I was officially opening a big carnival just outside Oxford. There I was, happy to sign autographs, try my luck knocking off one of the coconuts that I swear were screwed into their stand, try and shoot a fluffy duck, guess the weight of the cake, guess the weight of the lady mayor, whatever. Then suddenly the gushing voice of the local ladies' committee's answer to Mrs Hyacinth Bucket came trilling over the PA system.

'Would Mr Tarrant please make his way to the centre of the arena, where we're going to ask him to judge the entries to our beautiful baby competition.'

I wasn't in a position to refuse. But with hindsight I should have done. It didn't help that at that time I was single, had no kids that I knew of and didn't know one end of a baby from the other.

The biggest problem is, of course, that all mums think their baby is the best – by far the most intelligent and the most beautiful. To everyone else it may look like a barely formed blob with wind and sick at one end and I hesitate to name what at the other, but to the mum who went through all that pain to bring it into the world it is absolutely beautiful.

There are no real yardsticks to judge against, no hard and fast criteria to go by. It's hard to make any sort of comparison when they all look exactly the same. And how the hell do you judge a beauty contest when half the entrants are fast asleep, while the rest are bawling their little lungs out? If you get press-ganged into judging something like an under fives fancy dress competition you can usually get away with finding one with an 'aah' factor, but with babies they've all got an 'aah' factor. They're all dressed the same. Even the prams are more or less the same. Only the mums know the difference. I'm sure if you asked any of the dads to pick out their baby they wouldn't have a clue. It didn't help that none of the ladies on the committee would join me as co-judges, either. They obviously knew, from bitter experience, what a night-marish job it was.

'No, no, Chris,' they said. 'It must be entirely your choice. They're all so lovely.'

Gee, thanks ladies!

As I arrived there was a long line of prams awaiting my inspection, and a line of fiercely proud mums. Hyacinth gave me a microphone and pushed me into the fray. I was totally alone and totally terrified.

The babies were in three categories: the under eighteen months, the under twelve months and, daftest category of all, 0-six months.

I made a good start with the under eighteen months category. There was one particularly beautiful little Indian girl with a really shy mummy, so after much deliberation, I chose her.

Surely no one could object to that? Of course what

actually happened was that every single other mother objected to that. She was not only the prettiest little Asian baby in the competition, she was the only Asian baby in the competition, so I managed to upset absolutely everybody. There were sharp intakes of breath as I smilingly announced my choice. I don't think they were racist objections, the losing mothers just felt that an Indian baby had an unfair advantage. God knows why! I listened to the objections without understanding a single word and then, with my confidence draining away by the second, hurried on to the 'up to twelve months' class.

This one got really heated, with mums all around the ring shouting abuse at each other. I couldn't work out the reason for a lot of the aggro, but I have to say that is was a puzzle to me that one mum who had a baby in the under twelve months had already entered a separate and very different baby in the under eighteen months, minutes before. It is just about possible, but even my grasp of simple maths told me it was unlikely. There was then further uproar when the one that I chose turned out to be fourteen months old. One of the other mums remembered visiting the new mother and baby in hospital in May of the year before. It was now late August – well over a year later. More uproar, with a lot of shouting at the mum in question, a lot of heated abuse aimed at me and the committee: an outbreak of pram rage in general.

By the time I got to the under six months class – and they really did all look exactly the same – I just wanted to get out as fast as possible before the terrified army of mums nailed my private parts to the nearest elm tree. I

tried to look as if I was seriously considering which one of the little wailing Winston Churchills was the most beautiful but they all looked like a sea of bawling blobs to me. So I crossed myself and chose the blob in the third pram on the left.

An innocent choice, you would have thought, but again a very bad one. It never rains but it chucks it down. It turned out that the mother of the baby I'd chosen as the winner was the newly impregnated mistress of the bloke who's wife was the mother of one of the hotly fancied but rejected contenders in the under twelve months category. Dirty little devil. He'd been running round getting each and every one of them in the pudding club, and somehow I was getting all the blame. I admit that it wasn't the most diplomatic choice, but then if nobody gives you a bit of background, how the hell is a bloke supposed to know?

At this point the whole thing became a nightmare of outraged mums and mistresses using language that wouldn't have been out of place on a building site. As I thanked them all for having such beautiful babies and did a runner, one scandalized shouting mother knocked the splendid hat right off Hyacinth Bucket's head.

Needless to say, I've never been anywhere near a beautiful baby contest since, nor do I ever wish to! Don't misunderstand me: I've nothing against babies, just their beauty competitions.

Watching my own kids being born was probably the happiest and most fulfilling experience of my life. It's not for the squeamish, but I reckon if the woman you love can go through all that agony, the least you can do is be

there to hold her hand and try not to look as if you're about to faint.

The closest I got to passing out was when my little boy Toby was born. Ingrid had had a difficult pregnancy and birth and when the midwife pointed out the little bloodied head, and he screamed his little lungs out, we were all delighted that he had finally arrived, fit and well.

It was at this point that the distinctly manic midwife said to me, 'Would you like to see the placenta?'

I turned distinctly pale and had to hold on to the end of the bed for support.

'Er . . . no . . . it's very kind of you but, no, I really don't want to see the afterbirth, thank you,' I mumbled, absolutely horrified but trying not to appear ungrateful.

'Well I don't know what you're so worried about,' she went on. 'They're perfectly natural and healthy.'

Then, by way of extra assurance, she added, 'When Sting's wife has a new baby, the whole family eat the placenta at special organic dinner parties.'

I've no idea whether this is true or not, although I had heard a rumour about it once before – something to do with getting back to Mother Nature – and I've never been invited to dinner by Sting anyway, but I have to say it doesn't sound like my idea of a good night out.

Millions of babies are born every day. But there's still something about new life that makes people behave very oddly. The nation sussed that Prime Minister Margaret Thatcher had lost the plot entirely when she came running excitedly out of the maternity ward to announce, 'We are a grandmother!'

And I was once on an American radio station when their special guest of the day was the brilliant basketball player, Magic Johnson. Even for America, the arrival of Magic's new baby – Irvin III – was bizarre. Despite Magic being famous throughout the world as an Aids carrier there were apparently no problems with the pregnancy or the birth for his wife Cookie. As Magic told it, the only real problem, at the moment of Irvin III's delivery was Magic himself.

'I kept telling Cookie to push, saying things like, "come on – it's the fourth quarter, the game is tied, we need a basket, push, push!"

'Finally,' he said, 'the baby was imminent. Cookie was pushing like mad and I suddenly yelled, "Stop, everybody stop", and handed the doctors a CD to put in the CD player. It was a Luther Vandross CD because I wanted the first thing my baby heard to be a Luther Vandross love song.'

As if it's not bad enough being called Irvin the Third.

Just Some Pervert

One beautiful summer's evening at a nice little pool in Hertfordshire, I was packing up from fishing just as it was beginning to get dark.

I'd had a very successful day, caught a couple of seriously big fish, not seen another soul since early morning and was wandering contentedly back through the trees

listening to the bird song. As I rounded a little bush my reverie was broken by the sight of a girl's face. It was staring up at me in horror from the path, peering round the back of a man's head. Between the two of them they were wearing absolutely nothing. I don't know who was more surprised, them or me.

Without a word passing between us in the gathering dusk, they abruptly uncoupled – inflicting God knows what damage on each other – and not bothering to pick up any of their clothes, went rushing off up the path with their bits and pieces dangling out all over the place. Somewhere in the distance I heard a car start up and drive away, and if it wasn't for the little pile of clothes still lying on the path, I could have dreamt the whole thing.

Walking home quietly giggling to myself I wondered where on earth they'd gone to in that state, and what they'd say if they got stopped by the police. I had visions of the poor bloke giving it about an hour and then, still starkers, trying to sneak back, only to get caught by the extremely short-tempered gamekeeper with his equally nasty Doberman. I could see him crawling back to his lady, still naked, with a bottom full of buckshot and bites.

I thought no more about them until the weekend, when I returned to the lake for a spot more fishing. There, along the little path, piled exactly as they had been on the Tuesday, were the clothes. Jeans, jumper, bra, pants – just like before. Where that couple ever got to, or whether they ever got dressed again, I never found out. The clothes stayed there for another week and then the gamekeeper threw them on his bonfire.

It sounds bizarre. It is bizarre, but it's not an isolated incident. Far from it. One of the nicest things about fishing is that it gets you out and about in lovely, secluded places at a time of the day or night when there's usually no one else about. Still, misty dawns spent watching the sun rise over the mirror-like surface of a lake, or fiery-red sunsets as the heat of the day has gone and the night creatures emerge into the dusk are all part of the magic. And the silent, camouflaged angler shares them only with the herons, the foxes, the badgers . . . and couples getting their leg over.

Whenever I'm fishing, I seem to act like a magnet for courting couples. A dozen or more times over the years, I've been sat tucked away in some rushes by a remote pool with my little camouflage hat on when I've suddenly become aware of thrashing and grunting noises very close behind me.

Once I was so absorbed watching a big fish cruising about in front of me that the first thing that made me realize that I had company was something bumping against the side of my little fisherman's seat. I looked down and discovered a human foot. Naked, obviously female and pointing upwards. Sure enough, a couple of yards to its left was another one, and somewhere between the two was a nasty spotty bottom.

At such times it's difficult to know what to do. You can hardly jump up and tell them they're trespassing – you might rupture the pair of them. But you feel a bit of a voyeur if you stay put. I've tried coughing loudly but usually they're too far gone to hear or care. I've tried

a particularly deep, angry moo once, but all that did was make the young lady moan, 'Oh, you bull, you bull', to her man and start the whole business all over again.

I've come to the conclusion that you just have to try and concentrate on your fishing and hope that they'll go away. You also have to try very hard not to catch anything. I mean, how would you like it if you were peeled off, pleasuring or being pleasured in a cornfield and somebody swung a dripping, slimy bream past your ear. It would be very off-putting, and very likely to get the peeping Tom at the other end of the line a smack in the ear, thrown in – or both.

The problem is not confined to the banks. When I was about twenty I got myself settled down by one particular lake to fish through the night until breakfast time. But it was late September and the night was very cold and the fish didn't want to know. So about ten o'clock I decided to go and get a bit of kip in my car until first light. I'd parked in a nice little clearing in a wood, so I stretched the seat out, pulled a blanket over my head and was very soon well away.

Sometime just after eleven – coinciding, I suspect, with the local licensing hours – I was awoken by the noise of a car pulling into the little wood and parking alongside me. After a couple of minutes there was another. Then another. By about 11.30 there must have been at least forty cars surrounding me, all bouncing up and down on their shock absorbers. It was obviously the local lovers' hideaway – and it was about as discreet as the middle of Tottenham Court Road.

By 11.45 the night air over that little wood was filled with shouting and roaring, occasionally broken by manic laughter as some young show off stud attempted the physically impossible in an Austin Healey. One six foot plus local lad in a car behind me could obviously stand the bruising of his buttocks on the sunroof no longer and proceeded to straddle his lover across the bonnet. I tried not to peep, of course, but I did have a very good view of the soles of one of her feet in my wing mirror.

All this time, as a young guy of twenty with a newly awakened sexuality, I lay there under my blanket, in my wellies and smelling of fish, feeling terribly alone.

I prayed that at least one of the couples would have a violent disagreement and the angry girl would storm out of the car, looking for reassurance. I would have been across to her faster than you could say 'shoulder to cry on' but, of course, it didn't happen.

After midnight, the gasps and moans slowly died away. The occasional cigarette would glow through the darkness.

Engines were started up and one by one they melted away. By 2 a.m. it was as if it had never happened. An owl hooted the all clear and the moon came out.

Through my half-doze, I was vaguely aware of a car door opening somewhere close by. A blue light was flashing and then another light shone directly on my face through the window of my lonely little car. Then the footsteps began to recede.

I heard a deep voice say, 'Just one left, all on his own, George. Just some pervert.'

Love is in the Blood . . .

Ever since I was four, I've spent every spare minute of my life fishing. It's a total obsession with me; trout all through the spring, carp all summer and autumn, pike all through the winter and salmon whenever and wherever I can. It's a great relaxation, and by fishing early mornings at the crack of dawn, or a couple of hours in the evening, you can easily combine it with work. But you can't combine it with girls.

Every time I've tried to combine my love life with my much more serious (and much more successful) fishing life, it's been a disaster, and most disastrous of all was the bucket of blood.

Big fish are artful creatures and they get used to different baits quite quickly. They soon learn that certain baits have hooks in them and will leave that particular type of

food well alone in future. To combat this, we try all sorts of weird and wonderful baits to try and keep one step ahead. I think over the years I have put just about everything that's even vaguely edible on to a hook and chucked it into a lake somewhere. Bread, cheese, sweet corn, luncheon meat, liver sausage, paté, dog food, cat food, sardines, pilchards, turnips, carrots, broad beans, red beans, white beans, black beans, peas, chips, chunks of chicken, bits of turkey, chocolate, curry powder (it didn't catch anything but after a while a lot of bubbles came up), bacon, potatoes, plum cake, Christmas pudding, bird seed, semolina, cockles . . . I've tried the lot. Some have been very successful, some have been an absolute waste of time.

I even sat there once with a bit of cabbage on the end posing as bait, and because two of my mates had arrived, I was too embarrassed to wind it in and take it off, even though I didn't have a bite on it all day.

One of the best baits I came across was ox blood. It's not too easy to find, because there's been a shortage of oxen in the UK in recent years, but there's no doubt that if you can get some from a slaughter house, it definitely attracts certain types of fish from miles around.

It was the Saturday before the fishing season started on 16 June, and I'd made a fatal mistake. At a vital time of the year like that, when tackle's got to be prepared and worms have got to be collected in their thousands, I'd gone and fallen in love. For about three weeks I'd been dripping about like a great big lettuce, ringing her up, taking her out, drinking halves. I was really struck, but I knew we were coming up to a vital time of the year, when

nothing or no-one, however gorgeous, could keep me from living on a river bank. So I thought I'd give her a treat to keep her happy.

I'd promised to take her out for the day on the Saturday before the season started. I picked her up for lunch and she looked terrific. It was a baking hot day and she was wearing a bright yellow, low-cut mini-dress. She had really fair skin with a good suntan, blonde hair and beautifully white teeth. We had a totally blissful day. I bought her a really expensive lunch and then we just drove around in the country kissing and cuddling. Suddenly, late in the afternoon, I realized that the season was starting on Monday. Horrors – I'd forgotten the ox blood.

I couldn't take her with me to an abattoir. In fact, I couldn't even tell her where I was going. So I parked the car in the middle of town and said that I wouldn't be a minute, but I had to collect something for my mum. Before she could press me further, I dived off round the back streets to the slaughter house.

They were in full swing when I got there: ears, bits of liver and cows' goolies hanging up on hooks all over the place. I got one of those big plastic dustbins full of lovely steaming, congealing, frothing warm blood, gave the bloke a quid for letting me have it and another for helping me carry it back to the car.

For some unknown reason, my lovely lady didn't ask me why I had arrived back sweating and gasping accompanied by a bloke dressed like George Clooney from ER, wearing a surgical gown covered in blood and carrying a huge dustbin, which we dumped on the back seat. She

just looked at me in a puzzled way, asked, 'Got what your mum wanted?', and off we drove.

I'd cleaned up the bin and, with the windows open, you couldn't really smell anything, so we drove along happily enough with the radio playing rock 'n' roll and a lot of nibbling happening to my left ear.

Then, out of the corner of my eye I saw her . . . a little old lady of about eighty who walked up to the edge of a zebra crossing, decided to cross, changed her mind to let me pass, then changed her mind again and jumped out right in front of me. I stood on everything possible and screamed to a halt about three inches from her.

I don't know exactly how much lovely, steaming, congealing, frothing warm blood you can get into a plastic dustbin, but it's ever such a lot. There was a bit on the back of my coat and quite a lot on the window. But all the rest, gallons and gallons of it, was all over my new girlfriend. All down her plunging front, all over her yellow summer dress, all over her blonde hair, running down her legs. Everywhere you looked. It looked like a scene from The Godfather. Somebody very kindly asked if he should he ring for an ambulance, but I just drove off in a panic.

Her eyes peeping out of the fast congealing plasma were like two volcanoes. She was distinctly cross. She used words even I hadn't heard before. She screamed. She sobbed. She pummelled me. And me? I honestly tried to be comforting, but I just couldn't manage it. I had hysterics. The more she raged, the more I shook with helpless laughter. I kept saying, 'I'm sorry, honestly, I'm sorry',

but there were tears running down my cheeks and my lungs were absolutely bursting.

I woke up the next morning and got the giggles all over again. Needless to say, I woke up alone. Sadly, but not entirely unexpected, that was the last time I ever saw her.

On the Monday morning, I went fishing.

Stub It Out

One of the most successful, but extraordinary people I have ever worked with is Greg Dyke. He has a brilliant brain, a really wicked wit and a strong London accent with a voice that sounds not unlike Arthur Mullard having just swallowed a dishwasher.

Greg went on to become Chairman of ITV, which he eventually left with nine million quid in the bank, but when I first knew him he was producing the *Six O'clock Show* for London Weekend Television. Typically, he joined them as a researcher and within a matter of weeks was in charge of everybody. He had a mission to try and prove to a young, intelligent audience that current affairs could be fun and, in his hands, they sometimes really were.

We were the most unlikely set of bedfellows of all time. Headed by super smoothie Michael Aspel, there was also Janet Street Porter, Paula Yates, Samantha Fox, Fred Housegoe, Danny Baker and myself. Hardly an ego between the lot of us, I'm sure you'll agree!

It was a hugely successful programme and the next time I caught up with Greg he somehow blagged me into joining him when he took over as the incoming controller and saviour of the ailing TV-am. The famous five (David Frost, Angela Rippon and co.) had been and gone in a wave of adverse publicity in a matter of weeks. When I joined, as well as teaming up with my old mates from Central TV days in the Midlands, Nick Owen and Anne Diamond, the only other name they booked was broadcasting legend Roland Rat.

Between us all we somehow turned the station around. It hung on and even made a profit until 1993, when it lost its franchise and was replaced by the almost identical GMTV. By then, Greg and I had long since gone, and running things in Greg's place was Bruce Gyngell – an amiable but strange Australian whom I'd first worked with back in the Midlands in the seventies

when he was Lew Grade's number two in Birmingham.

I don't know quite what happened to Brucie while he'd been away down under, but when he resurfaced at the TV-am studios in Camden he wanted everybody to wear pink. He had had a plaque mounted in the foyer that said 'TV-am – the place to be. The winning team for 93'. As the staff came in to the foyer in the closing months of the station, they were all supposed to touch, rub or even kiss it and chant the slogan out loud and proud. Sadly they weren't the winning team and Eamonn and Anthea took over.

My twelve months at TV-am were in fact one of the best years of my working life. At any second the station seemed likely to go broke. Nobody got paid for months and months and there was no question of industrial action, let alone strikes, but the atmosphere among the crew, presenters and management was one of tremendous camaraderie, all pulling together just to survive another day. Miraculously, the thing stayed on air and, for a while, went from strength to strength.

One day when I'd quietly popped into the office to do my expenses – which were of course vast but perfectly reasonable – Greg came flying out of absolutely nowhere and grabbed me. Now, I must tell you that the extraordinary thing about Greg, other than being completely mad and using language that would make Billy Connolly blush, is that he is one of the greatest motivators of people I've ever met. Bear in mind also that I am six foot eight and that Greg is three foot seven.

He eyeballed me and said, 'Tarrant, I know it's your

day off but get out there. It's National No Smoking Day and TV-am wants you to champion our British "Stub It Out" campaign. Get a camera, get a fire bucket and grab a pair of scissors.'

With this, which is probably the most comprehensive and detailed brief I ever received from Greg, without a body guard or a safety net in sight, I went out on to the streets of King's Cross.

It seemed to me that I had every chance of getting a really good kicking, but I have to say that the collection of dinner ladies, commuters, prostitutes (we were in King's Cross, after all) and a lone wandering Franciscan monk that we encountered were all very reasonable. In fact the ridiculous thing was that they were too reasonable.

Greg's idea was for me to go up to complete strangers and say, 'Good morning Sir/Madam. It's National No Smoking Day and TV-am is mounting a "Stub It Out" campaign. I can't help but notice that you're smoking a cigarette. You can either stub it out in our bucket of sand or face the forfeit, which means that I will cut your cigarette in half with this here very sharp pair of scissors.' So these were their two choices.

In reality, there were actually a couple more.

Bearing in mind that this was being filmed first thing in the morning, they could carry on smoking their cigarette – which they were perfectly entitled to do – and walk away as fast as they possibly could, puffing happily, or they could smack me in the mouth. What was extraordinary about this item, which turned out to be a strangely watchable piece of TV, was that nobody went for options

c or d. They all clearly saw it as a straight neck and neck fight between option a and option b. Lots of them went for the bucket, several of them went for the scissors, but none of them went for the ignore or smack the flaxen haired fool in the mouth alternatives. What was really bizarre was that as everybody walked away from the camera, either with their cigarette doused by being stuck into my handily provided bucket of sand, or being completely ruined by me having cut it in half with my extra sharp scissors, every single person without exception turned smiling to camera and their last words were, 'Thank you!'

Thank you? What the hell for? It was your first and possibly only cigarette of the day and some gangling fool with a camera and a microphone cut it in half. Why on earth are you thanking him? I honestly think that if we set up a guillotine somewhere in central London and put a camera next to it somebody would be quite prepared to be the first person ever to be beheaded live on TV. As the head landed in the basket, it would turn on cue to camera and say, 'Thank you!'

I think it's all something to do with Warhol's fifteen minutes of fame, again.

The item was really rather good and I had begrudgingly to admit to Greg that it had been one of his better ideas. This, of course, was the worst possible thing I could have done because he said, 'Great – next week is the second week of the National No Smoking Campaign.' (I was sure it was only a one off thing but Greg was convinced that it was good for a fortnight, certainly as far as ratings were

concerned.) So on the spot he dreamed up 'Stub It Out – Part Two'.

'Hang on, Dykey,' I said to him. 'We've cut their cigarettes in half, we've stuffed them in buckets of sand, what the hell else can we do to these poor people who are happily enjoying what is probably one of the few pleasures left in their lives?'

'We'll take the forfeit a stage further,' says Greg, completely unmoved by any moral qualms or sheer cowardice on my behalf.

'What you need this time is a bucket of sand and a bucket of water. No scissors. No mercy.'

Seven days later I found myself back on the streets of King's Cross, again with no bodyguard, just a wimpy cameraman and an even wimpier sound recordist. This time between the three of us we were juggling a bucket of sand and a bucket of ice cold water. It was seven o'clock in the morning. People were going to work. They were not awake. They were not alert and, above all, they were not happy. They were probably enjoying their first cigarette of the day when suddenly they were confronted by a tall peroxide interviewer saying, 'Excuse me, my good man/woman. It's the continuation of "National Stub It Out Fortnight". You're on TV-am and you can either let us stub out your cigarette or pay the forfeit.'

As I said the words 'pay the forfeit' my brief was to leer ominously towards the bucket of cold water.

Most people, in fact nearly everybody, had the very good sense to stub their cigarette out in our bucket of sand and do a runner – presumably lighting up a second

cigarette as soon as they had got around the corner, hidden from the prying eyes of our camera. Again, the fact that they didn't actually have to do either of these options seemed to be forgotten. Nearly everybody went for the bucket of sand alternative. Nobody went for the carry on smoking and give me a fat lip possibility.

Only one gentlemen, a nicely dressed, clearly not particularly wide awake guy from Camden, failed to realize that the alternative between the bucket of sand and the bucket of water was really not an alternative at all. Either way, your cigarette would end up ruined. One way it was just your ciggie, the other way it was your ciggie, yourself and all of your clothes.

He went for option b.

'No, no,' he said. 'I don't see why I should do that. I'm not stubbing this cigarette out in your bucket.'

'Okay then, Sir,' I said to camera, 'I'm afraid you have

to pay the forfeit,' and I completely drenched him with a bucket of water.

This was a mere fifteen seconds, not fifteen minutes of fame and it consisted of a completely drenched man looking at me with murder clearly the only thing in his heart and in his blinking water-filled eyes.

Mister Rat Catcher Entertains

OTT, the late night show I produced in the early eighties, probably got more complaints than anything else I've ever done. Nudity, bad language, Alexei Sayle, Bernard Manning – it had all the ingredients of being thoroughly offensive to everybody. But – and this is so typically British – the biggest number of complaints didn't come in for offensive language or bare buttocks, but for an animal act!

Put an animal on the television and somebody somewhere will ring up to complain. In the course of your presenting duties you could get bitten by a tiger, but somebody would write to the broadcasting authorities about unnecessarily blunting animals' teeth. I couldn't, however, imagine people feeling sorry for rats. Not until I met Ken the Ratman. That was his job, down the sewer all day every day catching the nasty things.

It can't have been much of a job, but then Ken got this brilliant idea for supplementing his income: do a cabaret act with them. He would strip to the waist and

let them run all over his body. Better still, he would stuff them down his trousers. And best of all, he would stuff them down the front of a pair of tights so the audience could actually see them running up and down his leg. A totally new concept in club entertainment. Brilliant.

To say that bookings were on the thin side would be an understatement. People, in the main, didn't want to get their wife all dressed up with a new hairdo and sit her in the front row with a gin and tonic while some bloke paraded in front of her, stuffing rats down the front of his tights. Club managers, in the main, didn't rush to book him. But, when he did get a booking, Ken was sensational. He had to top the bill. Nobody could possibly follow him. Women fainted a lot and had to be brought round, and it certainly wasn't an act for anyone with a weak heart. It was a sensation.

When I first saw it, I couldn't actually believe what I was watching. People all around were screaming, half covering their eyes, their eyes behind their fingers wide open in utter horror. Yet, at the end, Ken received a standing ovation.

Great, thinks Tarrant. Scoop. I'll book him for *OTT*. After all, the show's supposed to make people sit up and take notice, isn't it? It's supposed to be totally unpredictable, to shock people. So we booked Ken for the next Saturday night.

It was probably the stupidest thing I've ever done.

The first problem was with Equity, the actors' union. Ken – surprise, surprise – was not a member and technically was supposed to be a member in order to appear on

television. So we had to have this ludicrous discussion with a very nice lady on the phone about what exactly his act consisted of, and whether or not, by using Ken, we would be 'depriving another actor of work'.

'Hello, Sir John Gielgud? Yes, got a nice little number for you at the weekend. Yes, three hundred quid. It's stuffing rats down your y-fronts. No, Sir John, it's not The Taming of the Shrew . . .'

Commonsense prevailed and Equity made Ken a member under the heading 'specialist entertainer'.

Saturday came. Rehearsals went fine. Ken did his stuff in time with the music, and the disbelieving crew applauded louder with each squealing little furry bundle that he popped down among his privates. Lenny Henry kept banging his head against the wall in hysterics.

'I don't believe it. I can't believe it. You're not serious.'

The big night. The piano played Ken's intro and in he came to face the unsuspecting audience. Stripped to the waist, his great paunch hanging over a specially-bought new pair of very see-through tights, he started to stuff the live, squealing rodents down his tackle box. The reaction in the studio was bedlam, complete uproar. One woman just stood on the top of her seat and screamed until long after the programme was over. Another bloke was laughing so much that he actually bit a great chunk out of the back of his hand and had to be rushed to the hospital, pouring blood.

In the middle of it all, with eight million people all over the country watching in spellbound horror, Ken's

nerve went. With about eleven or twelve rats already kicking and squealing about inside his tights and biting like mad because of all the noise and the hot lights, Ken dropped one.

As it raced around the feet of the screaming audience, Ken panicked. He swiped at it, tried to step on its tail and, eventually, in full colour close-up, gave it a great toe-ender back into its little box.

Ken had done something that until that moment I would have thought was quite impossible. He had managed to get people feeling sorry for rats. As we left the studio, the switchboard was jammed. I have never been able to understand the mentality of people who regularly ring to complain, and, on this particular night, we had some all-time classics. I can't really imagine what sort of person dials and dials and dials a television company until

after four in the morning, but that's exactly what happened.

The duty officer sat all night patiently logging each new complaint. As fast as he replaced the receiver another call came through. We were threatened with letters to the RSPCA, Mary Whitehouse, Lord Longford, questions in the House, the lot.

Nobody cared about poor old Ken's privates, bitten to shreds though they were. It was the rats that captured public sympathy.

My favourite quote from a very long and increasingly silly night was the still seething gentleman who finally got through to us at about 3.20 a.m. to dictate this message in all seriousness to our controller:

'Those magnificent animals should be free to roam the sewers, and not forced down any man's trousers . . .'

Grendel

One of the silliest jobs I ever had was being a security guard. Nothing silly about that in itself. The only really silly thing was that I ever got the job at all. It was at the time when security firms were very much a new idea, brought in from the States, and to get started, they seemed to take on almost anybody. In later years, security firms learnt some lessons the hard way and had to tighten up their screening. But when I joined a company for a summer job, they'd have taken on Ronnie Biggs.

'How tall are you?'

'Six foot two.'

'Can you drive?'

'Yes.'

'Got a licence?'

'Yes.'

'Had a photo taken in the last ten years?'

'Yes, in Woolworth's.'

'Okay, you start this afternoon.'

And that was it. The next day I was sitting with two complete strangers in the front seat of one of those big blue dormobiles with the chicken wire on the windows, and it was absolutely full of money. And I mean full. It was Friday. We had been right across the city collecting wages for all the major firms to pay out that afternoon. I don't know how much, but a long way into six figures, all in little bags in the back.

The older bloke says, 'Hang on here, lad, while we go and have a bacon sandwich.'

So there's me, an eighteen-year-old student who has just wandered in from Yates's Wine Lodge, all the keys in the ignition, sitting on something in excess of half a million quid, and my new boss is inside the greasy spoon deciding whether to have brown sauce or red.

At the time I thought that perhaps it's not as daft as it seems, it's a security test and they try out all new recruits in this way. After two days I knew it wasn't. It was like that all the time.

The next Monday I waited at the rear of Barclays with my little truncheon in my hand and another money box

chained to my wrist, standing guard over another one of my new senior colleagues who was busily pleasuring one of the married cashiers over a desk in an upstairs office. It had very little to do with security – it was just what they did on Mondays.

If you were on a night shift guarding a big factory or supermarket you were instructed to ring in every hour on the hour. If you didn't ring within three minutes of the hour, the place would soon be swarming with police cars.

Good idea, I thought, because I didn't fancy this night duty at all. Some of these big old Victorian factories were pretty scary at the best of times, and in the small hours of the morning any sudden noise was a definite trouser-filler. Ringing in every hour on the hour, that's more like security, I thought. Until the lads gave me my little egg timer.

'What's this?' I asked in total ignorance.

'It's an egg timer.'

'Yes – I can see that – but why do I need one? My shift finishes at six and I thought I could get a bacon sandwich in the cafe round the corner on my way home.'

'It's for ringing in.'

'Ringing in?'

'Yes. Set it for every fifty-nine minutes, get in your sleeping bag by the phone and then when it rings just lift the phone, give your name, say it's all quiet and go back to sleep.'

'Back to sleep?'

'Yeah. We've all got them.'

After a couple of nights on the job, I just took the

system for granted. I'd lie there all warm and snug in my blankets and pillows, and every time the egg timer sounded, without even opening my eyes, I'd lift the phone and say, 'Tarrant. Nice and quiet here', and go straight back to sleep.

Armed gangs could have blown the gate off, thrown in fire bombs, backed whole fleets of lorries right up to the factory entrance and emptied every warehouse, machine and conveyor belt in the place, but I'd have still dozed on oblivious in the security hut, with my little egg timer.

'Nice and quiet here.'

Then there were the dogs. I hadn't realized this before, but to get into the police force and go round legally biting people for double parking, dogs have to pass a special doggy exam. If they fail, they either go to one of the security firms or become chicken dansak. I expect (I certainly hope) that it's all changed now, but that was the system when I joined.

The dogs we got were absolutely hopeless. They were either too soft to be of use to anybody – they had no teeth and would keep turning over to let burglars tickle their tummies – or too savage to be trained. Of course, I got the latter type.

Grendel, it was called. Coal black with a temper like Adolf Hitler. It frightened the life out of me. I only had to do something provocative like try to put my hat on and it would go completely mental, barking and spitting at me in fury, nearly throttling itself with its own reinforced choke chain. There was absolutely no doubt in my mind that if it could get free, it would eat me.

As I set off very unhappily to start my shift with this rabid bear which I had to keep on a very short lead right next to my leg, the kindly old dog-handler – a man with ugly looking scars and stitches all over him – said to me reassuringly, 'Don't worry, lad, he'll only turn nasty if he can smell fear . . .'

Grendel must have had a damaged nose from biting armoured cars, because all night long I could certainly smell it, or something very much like it.

I managed to tie the wretched animal hard up against a filing cabinet on the far side of this big office while I tried to get my head down by the phone in the other corner. It was the longest night of my life. No need for the egg timer. I didn't sleep a wink for fear of waking up without a throat. That dog was an absolute menace.

The slightest noise, a cough or a match striking, and it would go absolutely berserk. At one point during the night the phone rang. It was some idiot with a wrong number, but by the time I'd got rid of them, the filing cabinet had moved about eight feet across the room towards me.

By the morning, when my relief came on at six, I'd had enough.

'I've got to go across town today,' I told him. 'Do me a favour and drop the dog off for me at lunch-time?'

'No problem, mate. What's it like?'

'Fine,' I said. 'Just give him a stroke and let him know you're his friend.'

As I was getting into my car, I heard a commotion like the outbreak of World War Three coming from the little security hut . . .

For Your Own Protection

When I was a student, my mate Ian and I set off for Spain in my car for a holiday in the sun. I had a bit of a run-in with an officious English policeman as we were zipping through Canterbury to catch the afternoon ferry. I was speeding a bit, but not a lot, but he was one of the bloody minded ones. Apart from the obvious pleasure he derived from nicking me for being eight miles over the speed limit, he went into seventh heaven when I explained we were hurrying as we were a bit late for the ferry. He did everything he could to make us miss it – although in the end, we caught it just as the only other remaining car was being loaded on.

I moaned about that copper all the way across the channel, all the way through France, and I think I was still

going on about him as we crossed the Pyrenees into northern Spain.

On the way down through Spain, Ian had been reading out an article in the Sunday Times about the number of students who disappeared without trace while on holiday in Spain. I hadn't really taken much notice. I'd been too busy raving on about my arrogant little chum with the pointed head.

As students with very long hair, jeans, T-shirts and a big flash car, we were just the sort of people the Spaniards absolutely hated. Or certainly the Basques. And that's where we were going, to the Basque country of the north-west, San Sebastian and Bilbao.

Two summers on Costa Brava camp-sites full of the English vomiting up paella, chips and Red Barrel had left us with no desire to go through it again. The two of us had decided that this year we'd try the other side of the country where there weren't supposed to be so many tourists.

That was an understatement. Apart from us, I don't think there were any, and it was pretty obvious why. We were totally unwelcome. The Spanish welcomed tourists but wanted them kept to the Costa Brava. To the Basques, we were about as welcome as the mumps.

It was little things that we noticed: the way people spat when we passed, the way we were left standing at the bar for more than half an hour before we could get a drink. We got the cold shoulder everywhere we went.

On the third evening we got attacked.

I'm over six foot tall and, in those days, I used to box

a bit, but I was no match for this bunch of mad, nationalist Spaniards. I was just locking the car up when about eight or ten blokes jumped on the pair of us, and within about five seconds I was rolling over and over on the ground covering my eyes with my arms while they took it in turns to put the boot in. And I mean boots, very big boots! Sometimes in my dreams I can still see them coming at me even now.

How Spain hasn't won the World Cup I can't understand. As this kicking continued, quite a large crowd built up, but nobody tried to stop what was happening. Through the haze I could see a Spanish policeman smiling down happily at the two human footballs in the market square. I couldn't believe it. I genuinely thought we were going to be lynched.

I'd seen those westerns where they break into the jail and drag out Clint Eastwood saying things like, 'Okay, American gringo, we're going to have us a little neck-tie party', but I'd never really thought it could happen to someone on their holidays.

Mercifully, it didn't . . . quite. After what seemed an age, but was probably less than five minutes, a second policeman arrived and between the pair of them they managed to talk this angry lot out of using my head for penalty practice and took me and Ian away to the nick.

'For your own protection, Senors. These men are very angry.'

Thanking them very gratefully we got into the police car and tried to piece together what on earth had happened. Presumably these two policemen would want some sort of description from us, even though they'd certainly seen the men themselves and would probably know them anyway. For the life of me, apart from the soles and toecaps of their boots, I couldn't really describe any of them.

It turned out not to be a problem. When we got into the police station an identification was the last thing they were worried about. They searched us thoroughly, even though all our money, watches, etc., were back with the gentlemen in the square. Then they motioned us to kneel in front of the desk.

I was a bit puzzled as to why we were doing this until the smallest and ugliest of them hit me over the head with a rubber truncheon.

'What the hell?' I said – only I didn't say hell – and jumped up, only to kneel back down again very quickly as his mate pointed a machine gun at my temple.

For the next fifteen or twenty minutes we both knelt on the floor as these two Spaniards took it in turns, very quietly and very methodically, to beat us unconscious.

The only really vivid memory I have of that police station is the enormous bottle of shampoo in the gents' toilets. It's just one of those things that sticks in your memory for ever. It was a huge, economy-size plastic container with something like 'Head and Shoulders' written on it in Spanish . . . I've always remembered because as they threw what was left of me into the cell, they made a point of washing my hair – presumably to get the blood out. The bottle was half empty.

We were left in that cell, bruised and dazed, not really comprehending what had happened. All the time with a real fear that we might never come out. If they decided to tell the Foreign Office that we simply hadn't ever come across the border, nobody in the world would know otherwise.

It was very frightening. Nobody spoke to us. We were grateful for the couple of appalling meals that were pushed under the door.

After two days, we were let out. Our car was returned to us and we were informed that we had been found guilty by the local court of causing the Spanish equivalent of a breach of the peace. We were fined – surprise, surprise – an amount that matched almost exactly the amount of money left in our case in the car and were told to leave the country within twenty-four hours.

We left that wonderful country inside twenty minutes.

We drove off the ferry at Dover battered and broke. There was a policeman doing traffic duty who, for some reason, made us halt the car and wind down the window. To his utter amazement, I stuck out my arm and shook his hand warmly and most sincerely.

The Raffle Ticket

I'm very good at taking holidays. It sounds obvious enough, but I'm amazed at how many colleagues of mine find it really hard to switch off. I know guys who will

ring me from the beach when they're supposed to be relaxing with the family, saying, 'Yes, I know I'm supposed to be on holiday, but I'm worried about that contract', or, 'Have you definitely booked the studio for Monday evening?'

I work hard in short bursts and then I stop. There's absolutely no in-between. I get on a plane, I pour myself a large drink and I completely switch off. No phones. No faxes. Nothing. I think I'm very lucky to be that way. It's probably a very good way of surviving in the frenetic and ridiculous world that I work in. My parents always have an emergency number for us and my agent usually has a number, but he's warned only ever to contact me on pain of death – or at least it had better be pretty damned urgent! In fairness to Paul, he's only ever rung me once on holiday in the twenty years I've been with him, and that was when LWT wanted an urgent answer about whether I'd take over from Clive James looking at weird TV shows from all around the world.

Clive had gone off to the BBC, Keith Floyd had been briefly tried and hadn't really enjoyed it – I don't think there was enough food and drink on the desk for Keith's liking – and they wanted me to take over. But they needed an answer before the weekend and I was away with my wife and kids for a fortnight.

I didn't need asking twice. It was a show I'd always watched and thoroughly enjoyed when Clive was doing it and I couldn't wait to take over. The deal was done over the phone and when I came back from my holiday I was wheeled straight into the viewing room to look at a moun-

tain of weird and wonderful clips from TV shows all around the world. I remember absolutely loving my first day and I've been loving it ever since.

The show is a very simple concept – a presenter at a desk with a monitor on top of it, with the clips that he's talking about coming up on the screen right alongside him. At first LWT wanted to call the new show *Tarrant With a Television* but when I pointed out to them that the initials of the show would be T.W.A.T they agreed that perhaps it was not a great idea and changed it to *Tarrant On TV*.

It's a refreshing show to make because no matter how savagely the critics berate the standard of British TV, the quality of our programme making still usually emerges as the best in the world. The range of shows that producers around the world pass off as entertainment is mind boggling.

The morning talk shows in America with the obligatory wild whooping audiences are utterly cringe-making and yet they are very hard to switch off. I am continually amazed by the people they manage to get into the studios and the sort of problems they are quite happy to discuss in front of an audience baying for blood and the millions of couch potatoes watching at home. In recent years I have seen a woman who was regularly having sex with both of her sons sit there in open forum with her husband, who only discovered the truth live on TV that very morning. I've seen a girl who had jilted her boyfriend because she'd fallen in love, not with his father – that would be too straightforward – but with his grandfather. And I've

seen an appalling New York Nazi taunt Jewish chat show host Jerry Springer that he had Jerry's mother, who had died in Auschwitz, outside in the boot of his car, skinned and made into a lampshade.

As I say, mind boggling stuff, and impossible to switch off, however tasteless and disturbing.

In LA they used to have a cable show called *The Gay Dating Game* which was exactly like the Cilla Black version, except that the host was a very large lesbian and the three hidden male contestants behind the screen answering questions like, 'Do you use your tongue when you kiss', would be talking to a man. They would then do the same routine with four girls. The Swedes, of course, being the Swedes, have their very own version of *Blind Date*. Again, it's exactly like our Cilla's version, except that in Sweden all the contestants are completely naked. Nakedness, as you might imagine is a regular feature on Swedish shows and pretty hideous some of the contestants are as well.

We also once ran an extract from a chat show in Spain where the host of the show was naked, and so were both of his guests. I was sitting there wondering what sort of audience would watch a show like this, when they cut to the studio audience and – surprise, surprise – they were all naked as well.

Meanwhile, back in the States, one of the great game shows of the late seventies was called *Dream Home* and in it you had a chance to win the house that you'd always wanted. To do so, husband and wife had to answer some pretty searching questions, including, 'Would you sleep

with a complete stranger for tonight's star prize?' Husband and wife seemed to agree quite happily that this was a good idea. Wifey disappeared for the night and the next day the house was theirs! It saved ever having to worry about the mortgage again but I can't help feeling that many marriages would have been put under tremendous strain by this rather bizarre pact with the TV devil.

It is one of a number of similar shows that disappeared from American screens with the arrival of Aids. Sleeping with complete strangers even for a 'dream home' was no longer felt to be a terrific idea.

In America they've been giving away thousands of dollars, dream homes, holidays in the sun and brand new cars for years. British game show prizes are rather cheap by comparison, with the obvious exception of the Lottery shows. We seem to be far more deregulated on radio than on commercial TV. I've been giving away £50,000 on the radio for several years now but have never been able to give away anything like that amount on British TV, which is a pity because if the programme makers can afford it, then why not?

In complete contrast to the Americans, the cheapest game show I ever saw came from Nigeria, where the star prize was a torch. In fairness I should add that it did include batteries!

Japan has its own special place in the hearts of TV viewers. It was Clive James who first brought the extraordinary Japanese show *Endurance* to British attention and Japanese television has formed a major part of the show ever since. Japanese TV shows are very different

from anything else you will ever see, anywhere else in the world.

Endurance was the most extraordinary affair. 10,000 contestants started out and there could be only one winner at the end of several gruelling weeks. No runners up. No booby prizes. Just 9,999 losers. And, the Japanese being Japanese, the shame of being a loser was almost too much to bear. The contestants were pushed to the point of exhaustion: their stomachs and their bladders at bursting point, force fed with everything from live eels to cockroaches and spiders, pummelled and beaten by all sorts of ingenious devices that would not have been out of place in a medieval torture chamber, even soaked in petrol and forced to run through hoops of fire. It was an amazing show. There's never really been anything else quite like it.

The other thing – and this is very rare on TV anywhere else in the world – is that the host of *Endurance* made no attempt whatsoever to get the audience or the contestants to like him. Throughout the whole humiliating process, the more the contestants suffered the more the grinning front man would berate them. The nastier it got, the more he would leer at the camera. If ever a man was in urgent need of a smack in the mouth, it was the host of *Endurance*, but perhaps that's why the producers chose him.

Japan and America may both seem geographically and culturally a long way away from Britain but it is amazing how very different even prime time European television can be from what we are used to this side of the channel. The French, until recently, ran a show where a fiancée

would come on blindfold and feel all over – and I do mean all over – a line of eager male contestants to see if she could pick out which one was her boyfriend. Invariably, she got the wrong one – to the embarrassment of the girl, the anger of the boyfriend and the delight of the audience and myself!

The French also ran a show starring a man in a loin cloth, whose particular talent was lifting very heavy rocks with his willy. The Fins chose a quite unspeakably tasteless sketch about the dos and don'ts of child molesting as their comedy entry for the Golden Rose of Montreux. Needless to say, it came easily last. And the Danes used a man in bed frantically trying to make love to a fast-deflating rubber doll as a commercial for puncture repair kits.

Most European countries have no qualms at all about using animals. Cats, dogs, even live chickens have all been used on one Italian Saturday night show in a way which, while not deliberately cruel, would certainly bring a storm of protest from outraged animal loving viewers in the UK.

There was a show running on Saturday nights in Holland that would certainly have caused public uproar if anyone was ever daft enough even to contemplate making it on British TV. It was a sort of people show that culminated with a live raffle – not exactly a very sophisticated idea, you'll agree. Since there was nothing so up-to-the-minute as an electronic scoreboard the winning numbers were chosen on good old cloakroom tickets. The only difference between this live TV raffle and any other raffle

that you've seen as the highlight of a Women's Institute summer fair was that in this case the winning ticket was hidden up a cow's backside – and the lucky, lucky contestant had to come and retrieve it . . .

The Champion

For the five years that I was supposedly a serious TV journalist, every night at six o'clock I would analyse the big stories of the day and occasionally read the news. My main job, however, seemed to be interviewing loonies. Our research team used to find them, drag them into the studios and every night I'd interview them. It's amazing just how many there are about: light bulb eaters, upside-down beer drinkers, flea trainers, hedgehog jugglers, men who ate live frogs, men who ate live slugs, men with

ferrets down their trousers, men with pigeons on their heads, men who ate live goldfish, men who slept up telegraph poles, women who knitted polo neck sweaters for poodles, women who'd met Martians in the chemist. There seemed to be an inexhaustible supply of them, and every night on the telly I had to try and get some sense out of one of them.

My all time favourite guest styled himself as 'the world champion egg, nose and water jumper'. I don't know where we found him but we should have left him there. The bloke was a very nice, very logical-sounding, one hundred per cent raving nutter. Completely out of his mind.

He was sixty-three years old, dressed in baggy knee-length football shorts, with particularly knobbly knees, a string vest and a huge pair of black boots, the soles of which he'd liberally plastered with boot polish. His props were an egg cup, a baby bath filled with water, a pile of sawdust and my nose. He had a really strong north-country accent and was at great pains to explain what he proposed to do.

'I shall need to borrow your nose,' he said, in all seriousness, 'and you'll need to by lying down. First, I shall slowly circumvent this standard chicken's egg placed here. At the right moment I shall hurl my body upwards just a fraction but enough to kiss the egg on the surface, marking it with the polish that I've placed on the soles of my boots, but without damaging the shell in any way whatsoever.'

I nodded eagerly. 'Can we make a start?'

'Aye, 'ang on lad,' he said. 'Just getting myself mentally attuned.'

This was all going out live, and was supposed to last an exact three and a half minutes, so we didn't have too much time for mental attuning. Still, I waited patiently while he stuck his head down between his baggy shorts, turned round, peered maniacally at me from up between his legs and let out a couple of whoops.

'All right, lad. Ready,' he said.

Before I could ask him what on earth whooping from between his legs had to do with anything, he did a series of mad bunny hops up to the egg cup and instead of lifting just a fraction off the ground, took off about four feet above it like a drunken wallaby.

'Just a bit high,' I said, helpfully.

'No, that was a good 'un,' he assured me. 'I just sort of caressed the top of the shell with both heels, lad.'

The gap between his heels and the egg could have let Concorde through, but not wanting to go through it again, and comprehending that I was in the presence of a five-star headcase, I nodded. 'Yes, just caressed the top of the shell,' and hurried him off across to the baby bath.

'Now, lad, I perfected this next bit as a result of studying the New Testament,' he announced, as he busied himself piling up sawdust for his next 'run up.'

I was about to mutter something about not remembering anything in the New Testament about Jesus walking across baby baths, but thought better of it and kept quiet. We could have been there all night if not.

'Watch carefully, lad, I'll take a good run up, check my

body and then with a sort of half-walking, half-skating motion, take four steps across the water without disturbing the surface.'

At this point there was a distinct snort from behind one of the cameras and, taking a quick look round as this madman was doing the whooping between his legs routine again, I realized that people were starting to get the giggles. But in the far corner of the studio I could see a well known, particularly pompous MP who was due to be interviewed as soon as I could get this raving loony off. With the usual politician's sharp sense of good fun, he was scowling and frowning.

It's getting out of hand, I thought, and turned back just in time to see the champion go roaring up to the water jump and, instead of doing the promised four steps across the surface, go skidding wildly on the sawdust and knock the baby bath flying across the floor.

The studio erupted.

There was a great bark of, 'Oh, for God's sake' from the prominent MP and I gurgled out something like, 'Well, let's leave the water' and went and lay down on the studio floor ready for the Nose Jump.

'Nay, lad, I can't do the nose until I've done the water,' said our hero, and I had to suffer the indignity of getting back up again, my back covered in boot polish which he was distributing liberally around the studio floor. I stood by like a giggling jelly while buckets were brought and the baby bath was refilled. There were more whoops from his head jammed down between his legs and then he raced up to the bath. With some strange long-jumper scissor

kicks in mid air, he cleared it by a great margin. He was nowhere near the water. Not that he seemed to know any different. As he landed on the far side of the baby bath, he let out a great triumphal victory shout of 'Done it' and rushed back and forth around me, punching the air with his fist like Eric Cantona winning the FA Cup.

It was complete chaos. The floor was covered in Cherry Blossom boot polish, the director was screaming obscenities through people's headphones, one of the cameramen was holding his ribs and trying to draw breath in great gulps, the MP was hissing with rage at the floor manager and I had completely lost it. I went and lay down again, nose at the ready, sobbing with laughter.

'For God's sake, don't laugh, lad,' he barked at me in total seriousness which only made we worse, 'or one of us could be killed!'

I lay there on my back, desperately trying to keep my nose still, howling with laughter. With eyes closed, I heard the whoops again from somewhere down between his knobbly knees. There were a couple of heavy bootfalls from just beside one ear, and then there was a great thump on the end of my nose, followed by the whole Eric Cantona routine all over again.

My nose felt as if it had been hit with a shovel. It was pouring a mixture of blood and boot polish. Somehow, with the champion still fanning the air in triumph and the strains of 'You'll Never Walk Alone' that the director had added as a finishing touch filtering through in the background, I thanked the egg, nose and water jumper and roared off to see the nurse.

The interview had been scheduled for three and a half minutes and took just over eleven. And the MP had to come back again the next day.

Radio Days

In 1984, when I first came to work in London, I was still contracted to Central Television, was still living in the Midlands and had no real knowledge of Capital Radio at all. I knew Mike Aspel and Kenny Everett socially but all I really knew about Capital was that it was a place that Kenny used to post his weekly Saturday show to somewhere in London. In those days he lived not far from me in the Cotswolds in an old converted pub with his own built-in studio in the basement and he used to make his brilliant weekend show, Captain Kremlin and all, and send it off on Wednesdays from the little post box on the corner of his road.

Presumably Kenny kept some sort of master copy in his house but he used to say, 'Here it comes, darlings – another masterpiece!' and pop it in the post-box.

Capital was the first radio station I'd ever worked in and I've been there ever since. I was struck immediately by what simple instant fun you could have on radio.

Although the ludicrous over-manning that used to happen on all TV programmes has largely ended, I still tend to arrive in a TV studio to find an army of people rushing about clutching clipboards, each pretending to have a very

important job to do. Usually the series is over, and they've all left before you ever did find out who they were and what the hell it was that they did.

Radio is the best fun. Live radio remains a small, intimate medium, very much a live medium and much the better for it. As television becomes more and more pre-packaged, over-dubbed and recorded in cost effective blocks, live radio remains more honest and much more fun to work in. You can still have a good idea at 6.15 in the morning and do it live on air at 6.35. You can also realize by 6.40 that it was a bloody stupid idea, and try and pretend that it never happened. The great thing about doing anything, however disastrous, at 6.35 in the morning, is that none of the management will have heard it!

These days, I much prefer working on radio. I'm much better looking on radio and I feel all together more at home.

I'll give you an example of how television has changed. A very close producer mate of mine was working with me on a series I recently recorded for ITV, and in all seriousness one afternoon during rehearsals he said, 'Okay, Chris, you'll make your entrance through this archway here, the camera's over there. Now, what's your first ad lib going to be?'

How the hell did I know? Isn't that the whole point of ad libs?

Like everybody, I have my own list of radio heroes, and over the years it's become quite a long one, but they would include Kenny Everett, probably the best disc

jockey of all time, Noel Edmonds, when he did the breakfast show on Radio One, Michael Aspel, Steve Wright, Les Ross, the late Ray Moore, Steve Penk, Terry Wogan and Roger Scott.

Roger was tremendously knowledgeable about music and was a fanatical Bruce Springsteen fan. He had a collection of every record that Springsteen had ever made, and went to see him whenever he was performing, almost anywhere in the world.

To illustrate how much music policies have changed on almost all stations these days, on the day that Springsteen brought out his three hour Live at Wembley album, Roger – who used to follow my show in those days – went into the studio, turned up all the speakers and played the whole three hour album non-stop for the entire duration of his three hour show. I like Springsteen. Lots of people like Springsteen. But three hours seems a little excessive to say the least. After about an hour and a half even Bruce would have been desperately trying to find another radio station to listen to.

I remember when I first heard a phone-in in the States. I was impressed by how many nutters there were on their morning phone-in and wished that we could find a few of those sort of people in London. What I soon realized when I joined Capital was that London has got even more nutters per square inch than New York, and they'd all just been waiting for their own little radio home.

Over the years, the most extraordinary people have rung me up to tell me the most extraordinary things. One guy called Andy rang up in all seriousness one morning

to tell me how much he loved the M25! 'Going on to the M25 is like going to a West End play,' he said. 'We should enjoy it and be grateful for it.' I can imagine that call going down a storm with all the commuters actually sitting stuck in jams all the way round the dreadful thing!

Another guy rang up to ask me to replace his radio because he'd been caught by his girlfriend making love to another woman on a pile of coats at a party and when he got home all his furniture, including his radio, had been thrown out of the window. The radio was smashed to pieces.

Another woman told me that she called her car 'Willy', ''Cos he's little and cute and I like him.'

We used to do an item called 'Party Pieces', which was quite an eye opener as to the lengths people would go to to make complete fools of themselves on the radio, particularly first thing in the morning. We had all sorts of people performing the most amazing feats including jumping off a wardrobe, pretending to be a racing motorbike and roaring round their bedroom running over their brother's foot in the process, and doing handstands while singing Rule Britannia.

All this was on the phone, on the radio, and it says a lot about the worrying state of our nation. I never really want to know who I'm going to be talking to or what they want to talk about. I like walking into the unknown. My producers, Titch and Annie, deliberately never give me any sort of briefing. They just say, 'There's a really good loony on line three.'

A guy rang me one morning and said that he wanted

to jump out of his window on the count of three and land on the tarpaulin roof of a market stall underneath.

I said, 'Okay, Dave, you're on your own, pal.'

I gave him a count of 'three, two, one' and from the dying scream and the thud that came down the telephone line it was obvious he really had gone and done it.

I played a jingle, went to a record and forgot all about it. About ten minutes later an irate market trader from Bethnal Green was shouting abuse at me over the airwaves.

'Some prat has just jumped through the roof of my market pitch and he said that Chris Tarrant had put him up to it.'

The other thing I've discovered is that people are incredibly gullible first thing in the morning.

On April Fool's Day in recent years we've done all sorts of things and, because people aren't at their most alert at the crack of dawn, they've fallen for it hook, line and sinker.

I did a ridiculous stunt years ago with Richard Branson, who went up in a green hot air balloon with strange flashing lights just before daylight.

We started the ball rolling with one or two deliberately placed calls from the Oxfordshire area, from where Branson had set off. Within a matter of minutes extraordinarily gullible people were ringing up and telling us that the aliens had landed, that they'd definitely seen this spacecraft in parts of Essex and Kent – even though we knew for a fact that Branson was at least a hundred miles away. The whole thing came to a disappointing halt when

Richard and his balloon went meandering across a busy motorway causing chaos and panic among the motorists underneath. The boys in blue weren't terribly impressed by the idea and he had to land hastily.

I once announced on air that I'd been away on a course in a commune in the West Country and had found the meaning of life, man. We set up a love and peace mantra line and told people that if they wanted to change their lives, they could ring in to the line and we would take their message. When they rang through, we told them that it was April the first and they'd been had. It sounds a silly, weak idea, but over 14,000 people rang in that morning!

The most successful prank of all, and perhaps the simplest idea, was April Fool's Day 1995, which fell on a Saturday. We thought, what a wacky wheeze it would be to come in on the Saturday morning, normal time, send up the Flying Eye, etc, and tell everybody it was Friday 31 March.

I remember at the ideas meeting someone said, 'Oh, come on, nobody will fall for that.'

And we argued, 'First thing in the morning, oh yes they will!'

We had hundreds and hundreds of calls from people who were thoroughly confused! People are so gullible first thing in the morning. If the nice man on Capital tells you that it's Friday, then it's Friday, even though, when you opened your eyes, you were sure it was Saturday.

One bloke with a terrible hangover from his weekly Friday night booze-up got as far as the bathroom, con-

vinced it was Friday again. A woman set off for a meeting she'd already had the day before!

Another woman drove in to her London office from Gerrards Cross. It crossed her mind that the Friday morning traffic was a bit light, and was pleasantly surprised to find a lot more room than usual in the car park. She sat alone for an hour in her big open-plan insurance office, just along the Euston Road, where there were normally 3,000 people working, before she realized that she'd been had!

The Wrong Nelson

Danny Baker and I always used to draw lots to see who would do the outside broadcast on LWT's Six O'clock Show. It wasn't that either of us wanted to do them, quite the reverse. We both absolutely hated it and yet one of us would get stuck with the job each week.

Michael Aspel would sit in the nice, warm studio at his nice, comfy desk and one of us would be stuck out in the middle of absolutely nowhere, probably in driving rain or sleet, desperately trying to sound excited about an outbreak of Weil's disease in Romford, or worm charming on Wandsworth Common. The broadcast usually consisted of a drive of up to two hours each way for an item that was frequently less than a minute. If the show was running over, it was invariably the first item cut down in time. A live show with guests always ran over and I remember

doing an item which was scheduled for two and a half minutes when I left in the afternoon and was down to thirty seconds when I phoned in having got to the location!

If you've ever seen the enormous amount of trucks and cables and manpower that arrives with the average outside broadcast unit, you can appreciate that taking all that lot anywhere for an item that only lasts thirty seconds on screen isn't particularly cost effective.

It wasn't just the sheer dullness of lots of the stories that got Danny and I down, it was missing out on the free drink after the show. Mr Smoothie Michael Aspel, the rest of the presenters and any celebrity guests would dive into the hospitality room as soon as we came off air at seven o'clock and proceed to get absolutely legless. Whoever was stuck on the outside broadcast would come crawling back to base at about nine, by which time the whole place was locked up and in darkness, without a drink in sight.

My first ever outside broadcast, years earlier, from Dudley Zoo, was infinitely worse than anything the *Six O'clock Show* could offer. As soon as I introduced the show with, 'Hello, good evening and welcome to ATV today, coming to you live tonight from the zoo here at Dudley in Worcestershire', a particularly bad tempered orang-utan in an enclosure immediately behind me started to pelt me in the back of the neck, with uncanny accuracy, with great mounds of fresh ape dung. I don't know how much they'd fed that orang-utan that day, but he seemed to have done mountains of it. He had an inexhaustible

supply and kept this routine up for the entire programme every time I opened my mouth to say something to the cameras. He'd obviously seen some of my work before and was speaking for lots of viewers!

When I got back to base for a clean up after the show, my producer said, 'I'm sorry about the orang-utan, Chris, but trust me – it was funny and it looked great in colour.'

Radio outside broadcasts, on the other hand, have in the main been great fun and have enabled the Capital breakfast show team to see almost every corner of the world in recent years. We've come live from Australia, Los Angeles, Hawaii, New York, South Africa, Kenya and just about every holiday resort in Europe, including several splendid weeks from luxury yachts moored along the Riviera. It's been hell!

The first one I ever did wasn't quite so much fun. We did the breakfast show live in Tenerife, starting at 5.30 in the morning. At 5.30 in the morning, everybody in Playa de Las Americas has been up all night clubbing and drinking and is still absolutely legless. This huge audience of British drunks came straight out of the various clubs to see us in action and by the time we went on air they were feeling no pain whatsoever.

As I said, 'This is Capital breakfast on 95.8 FM – live from Tenerife', there was a huge drunken cheer from the assembled throng and a can of McEwans hit me squarely on the head, obviously thrown by some relative of the orang-utan at Dudley Zoo.

The first hour of the show was absolute chaos with a

lot of very unfriendly Spanish policemen with sub-machine guns looking increasingly menacing towards the crowd. Eventually, however, they all slowly started to wilt and by about seven o'clock were lying fast asleep all around us in the morning sunshine.

One of the problems about doing outside broadcasts from exotic places, particularly in the winter, is that if you're not careful you can really cheese people off. The last thing I would want to hear if I was stuck in a traffic jam on the M25 on an icy January morning would be some cocky DJ telling me how nice and sunny it is in the southern hemisphere.

I remember the first time we came live from Sydney. A huge crowd of Brits turned out to see us. It was evening over there, and the end of a baking hot February day. Every time we read out the English weather, which was minus four and absolutely freezing, they all let out a huge cheer, as if to say, 'So long, suckers – we're in the right place!'

We've had some great shows from Australia. It's a fabulous country, the Australians themselves are always very hospitable and, of course, the extra bonus is that you do a breakfast show at tea time. We usually go on air at something like 5.30 p.m. – after lunch, a couple of beers and a swim – and it seems to me a much more civilized way to do a breakfast show, particularly in the middle of February.

But it's not always sunshine. Once, in the middle of the Australian Bush, about 300 miles inland from Sydney, we copped for one of the most spectacular storms I can

ever remember. It was a beautiful sunny evening when we went on air but within half an hour the wind had approached something close to gale force and the rain was coming across our turntables and equipment from the side.

It was one of the most ridiculous shows I can ever remember. It was so wet that we got the giggles. Wild Australian rock 'n' roller Jimmy Barnes was supposed to do a live number for us which, to his eternal credit, he did, but he had to use an acoustic guitar because with the rain pouring all around us, his electric guitar would have been an instant death trap.

At one point I remember seeing my entire script and running order washing away down a drain, and all the labels on the records washed away, so that a lot of the time we had no idea what the next record was called until it came on. We may well have played the same record three times.

During that trip we also came live from Hobart, Tasmania, which is a beautiful place. On the morning we were there they were a little bit thin on news to say the least. We tried to do some street interviews but there was absolutely nobody in sight. The front page lead story on that day's *Hobart Chronicle* was 'bicycle stolen from outside supermarket'!

We had a fabulous trip to Cape Town. I'd never been to South Africa before, for obvious political reasons, but after the abolition of apartheid it seemed an interesting place to visit. It proved to be one of the most beautiful countries on earth. We interviewed lots of English people who had moved out there because life and property is so incredibly cheap. We toured the vineyards and guested on a couple of radio stations.

There was one memorable moment on the local Good Morning Cape Town hip hop breakfast show, when me and Howard Hughes, my staggeringly daft news reporter, were being interviewed by a fairly serious local presenter who asked us, 'What do you people in Britain really think about Nelson?'

Howard jumped in, saying, 'Oh, we have tremendous respect for him. He really is quite a hero to all of us. There's a great big monument to him in London in the middle of Trafalgar Square and we all think of him as one of the greatest naval commanders of all time.'

The DJ looked at Howard gobsmacked. I kicked him several times on the shins under the table and eventually had to point out to him that if we were asked in South Africa about our views on Nelson, chances were that we were talking about Mr Mandela!

We have done several shows from America, New York, Florida and Los Angeles. The big problem over in the States is that it's completely the other side of the world from Australia and you end up doing breakfast shows in the middle of the night. In LA we went on air at eleven o'clock in the evening and it really wasn't a good idea to be doing live street interviews at 1 a.m. in the middle of drug gang territory, which is where the studios were. After one false start on our first show, when we were politely escorted back in by a kindly sheriff, we stayed indoors with the door locked.

Getting guests to come along at two in the morning is not easy, so the second night we thought we'd come live from a place called the China Club, right in the middle of the city. This was a much better idea. The atmosphere was great and there were lots of people to interview, including a number of celebrities. It was one of the most popular clubs in town and the night we were there Rod Stewart was around, John Travolta popped in, along with a couple of the Doobie Brothers and country star Kenny Rogers.

Kenny was in there with a load of friends and some enormous minders celebrating his fiftieth birthday. He is

probably one of the richest men in America, having sold millions of albums, and was in a great mood. I interviewed him on the show, wished him a happy fiftieth birthday and then a couple of our crew and myself tried to give him the bumps.

Kenny is a very nice, easy going kind of a guy, but apparently in the States, they don't have a tradition of giving people the bumps on their birthdays. In fact, they had no idea what I was doing and decided I was dangerously mad. Five or six enormous bodyguards dragged me off him, emphasizing very strongly to me that the interview was over and that we'd better put Mr Rogers down in a hurry.

New Toilet Duck

I remember the day I did my first voice-over for a TV commercial. I had to say 'Smiths crisps, every potato wants to be one' lots of times until they decided on the best one. Just fifteen minutes' work and I went away quite a few quid richer, thinking this is the life for me!

Since then I must have done hundreds and hundreds of voice-overs, and I've always thought it's the best-paid job in the world, requiring the least amount of effort, or, in the main, talent. Considering the longest booking you're ever likely to get is an hour and usually the job's finished well inside of that, it really is a bit of a breeze.

In the words of the late Brian Glover, who did all sorts

of commercials for years and years (he's probably best known as the voice of Tetley's Bitter), 'It's not a fortune, but it is half a fortune.'

Some people have made enormous sums of money out of their voices. Lots of much respected actors are quite happy to extol the virtues of cat food, cornflakes or condoms as a lucrative way of whiling away the time until they're next booked to play in Hamlet. Ian Holm, Robert Powell, Anthony Valentine, even Sir Michael Horden have all been lured into the world of the commercial makers.

Some actors would go pale if their agent found them six weeks' solid stage work as it could seriously disrupt their voice-over availability and their earning potential.

For a while I was very much the flavour of the month and it happens to a lot of people. In my case, it was purely because I was a familiar voice that was constantly being heard in London on the radio. At the height of that period, it became a little ridiculous. I remember one commercial break on ITV one evening which had five different commercials in it and my voice was used on all five. When it gets like that it's downright silly and, of course, the bubble bursts.

It's something that everyone accepts. There was a period when every voice on every commercial belonged to my fishing mate Patrick Allen. Kenny Everett did hundreds for a couple of years. So did Ray Brooks, Hywel Bennett, David Jason, Geoffrey Palmer, Tommy Vance, Angus Deayton, Michael Jason and Ian McShane. They all went through the 'flavour of the month' routine and then went quietly back into just the occasional booking.

Nick Hancock was probably the most used voice of 1997.

There are other guys and one or two girls who really do make serious money by just having a great range of voices and the real bonus going for them is that they're not particularly well known. They're just very good and can be used time and time again without anybody outside advertising circles knowing who they are.

You can see them regularly in the streets of Soho with their bleepers going off telling them of their next booking. They have their own voice-over agents with names like Voicebox, Hobson's Choice and Deep Throat. The whole thing has become a very serious business.

Over the years I've advertised everything from Mazda cars, Crown paints, Walker's crisps, Smith's crisps, Access cards, Breakaway chocolate bars, Kellogg's Fruit and Fibre, Liquorice Allsorts, Bold washing powder – to my all time favourite, at the peak of my career, New Toilet Duck!

That was the day that I realized I'd finally sold my soul and I didn't care. It's a heady feeling when you can get home and say proudly to your wife, 'Great news, darling – I'm the voice of Toilet Duck!'

I remember once when I was still commuting to London from Warwickshire that I got home late one evening after a busy day. There was nothing in the book for the next day and I was looking forward to a nice day off, but when I got indoors the answer phone light was flashing and there was a message for me to ring Paul, my agent.

When I got hold of him, he said, 'I had to book a voice-over for you at nine o'clock tomorrow morning.'

I said to him that I really wasn't too keen, I was fairly knackered and I really could do without racing back down to London early the next morning.

'Sorry,' he said, 'but I had to book it – the client is apparently a great fan of yours and the whole commercial has been written very much in a Tarrant style to fit your sense of humour.'

'Okay,' I said, 'it sounds like fun. I'll be there.'

So the next morning, having blasted back down the motorway, I got to the studio bang on nine o'clock and sat excited and intrigued to see what the scriptwriter had come up with to suit my peculiar style.

The advert was for a furniture sale and you can imagine my surprise when the writer came in with the script in his hand, like Moses coming down the mountain with the Tablets, and there on the page was what I had to do and what I'd come racing down the motorway for. Just three words. 'Don't miss it!'

I have no idea why they so desperately needed to book me, but I gave them the performance of a lifetime with about fifteen different alternatives and ten minutes later was back in my car heading north again up the M1.

Freak Or Unique?

The Chris Evans Story

David Jones

Channel 4's *The Big Breakfast* brought Chris Evans stardom, which he has since sealed with the success of his own TV shows, *Don't Forget Your Toothbrush* and *TFI Friday*. To his millions of fans he is a comic genius, the essence of popular culture. His trademark off-the-cuff humour and shocking irreverence have established him as the most gifted broadcaster of his day, but to his detractors he is a lewd, arrogant egotist.

How did the bullied child become a notorious bully? How did the devoted son become the father who never sees his own daughter? Full of contradiction, but endlessly fascinating, the name of Chris Evans never fails to spark fierce debate. *Freak Or Unique? The Chris Evans Story* talks to the people who have loved and hated him over the years and tells you everything you want to know about the man behind the glasses.

ISBN 0 00 653017 6

Wannabe A Spice Girl?

A Beginner's Guide to Girl Power!

Mark Leigh and Mike Lepine

Do you have what it takes to be a Spice Girl? Do you *know* what it takes to be a Spice Girl? The Spice Girls are Britain's biggest single export earner after spent plutonium fuel rods and infected beef carcasses. Wouldn't you like to be a part of it?

Only this book takes you into the Spice-O-Sphere and shows you:

- How to apply to join the group
- How to write songs as good as the Spice Girls
- How to love your mum the Spice Girl way
- How to express your individuality – and be just like your favourite Spice
- How to attract a hunky Premier League soccer star of your very own

Don't be fooled into joining those sad imitations, like The Rice Girls ('Pilau' Rice, 'Brown' Rice and 'Uncle Ben's' Rice and their friends will never make it big . . .) – go straight to the top with *Wannabe A Spice Girl?*

If you only ever read one book in your entire life . . . you're a perfect candidate to join the group! So come on in! Live the life! Dream the dream! And make the money!

ISBN 0 00 653028 1

He Died With A Felafel In His Hand

Hilarious True Stories of House-Sharing Hell

John Birmingham

'You'll read it with horrified amusement and, if you've ever shared a flat, the occasional wince of recollection.'

TERRY PRATCHETT

'A rat died in the living room at King Street and we didn't know. There was at least six inches of compacted rubbish between our feet and the floor. Old Ratty must have crawled in there and died of pleasure. a visitor uncovered him while groping around for a beer.'

So you think your flatmates are from Hell? Never clean up after themselves? Sometimes forget to flush the toilet? But did they ever run up a £20,000-credit scam from home? Ever blow up a perfectly innocent milk van? Or bring a stampede of corrupt police through your door?

John Birmingham's did. And he secretly took notes on all of them. 89 flatmates later, this is his very funny story.

ISBN 0 00 638857 4

99 More Unuseless Japanese Inventions

Kenji Kawakami

Translated by Dan Papia

There can never be enough gadgets to help solve the niggling problems of modern life. Back by popular demand, *99 More Unuseless Japanese Inventions* brings more brilliant and bizarre gizmos to an unsuspecting world. With the logic-defying, deliciously nonsensical Japanese cult of Chindogu, life will never be the same again.

- Keep dry and fashionable with the Stormy Sky Tie. Wear it around your neck, or above your head.
- Kiss goodbye to smudged lipstick by using the Smearless Lip Stencil. Just place it over your mouth and fill in the gaps.
- You'll never lose your umbrella again, and you'll always have your hands free, if you have an Umbrella Hat.

This is the book that will change your life for ever!

ISBN 0 00 638897 3